HUMANS AND THE ENVIRONMENT

Understanding This Complex Relationship

By Dr. Adrian James Tan

Southern Methodist University

San Diego, CA

First published in the United States of America in 2012 by Cognella, a division of University Readers, Inc.

16 15 14 13 12   1 2 3 4 5

Printed in the United States of America

ISBN: 978-1-60927-810-6

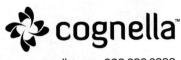

www.cognella.com 800.200.3908

Contents

Preface   vii

What Is Sociology?   1

The Origins of Society   9

Research Methods   19

Sociological Theories   31

The Environment and Population   37

Social-Cultural Evolution of Societies   45

Pastoral (Pastoral-Nomadic) Societies   55

Agricultural (Agrarian) Societies   61

The Advent of the Modern World   73

Karl Marx (1818–1883)   89

Karl Emil Maximilian Weber (1864–1920)   99

Emile Durkheim (1858–1917)   107

Georg Simmel (1858–1918)   113

Global Stratification 119

Globalization 127

The Social-Cultural Evolution Revisited 133

Bibliography 137

I dedicate this project to my wife, Swee-Lian, and son, Brandon, for their unconditional support. This effort is for the two of you. I am also grateful to my schoolmates, Gerard Goh and Jerome Lim, and my friend, Rory Leidelmeyer, for allowing me to use their pictures in this project.

Preface

Over the years, in teaching Introduction to Sociology classes, I had a hard time grappling with traditional textbooks, which were (and still are) encyclopedic in nature. Though rich in details and filled with vital information, teaching the course became cumbersome and challenging. Students were bombarded with a volley of information, and many chose to remember the information by heart, rather than understanding the message relayed. This defeats the purpose of learning.

From an instructor's standpoint, they were scripts that were difficult to follow, and it was a challenge to maintain flow and continuity from one topic to the next. There was the absence of a theme, and teaching from it was like delivering pieces of a jigsaw puzzle without showing students the entire picture. What made it more difficult was that some institutions implemented standardized texts, stifling whatever potential the instructor had in delivering the best message possible.

From the student's perspective, reading from encyclopedic textbooks was monotonous, and at times the books were hard to follow. Students felt bombarded by the multiplicity of information, which they found fragmented and repetitive. To them, it was difficult to get into the substance of the subject matter, as the chapters provided extraneous information through superficial, long-winded discussions. The students became bored easily—inadvertently, reading became a painful experience.

In order to alleviate the problem, I incorporated several books into my courses, tying common denominators among all of them. To be honest, I was apprehensive at first, but as time progressed, my courses developed a "personality," and a theme gradually developed. Most serious students initially found the readings hard to follow, but reached their "Eureka!" moments by mid-semester. It is based on my years of developing a theme that I came up with this book.

The purpose of this book is to offer the reader a simple, direct approach to sociology. Unlike most sociology textbooks, this book does not barrage the reader with facts and discussions of the numerous social issues in question. Instead, the discussion follows a theme, consistent with a theoretical approach. It tells a story and develops the plot as each chapter progresses.

Following a theoretical perspective modeled on Gerhard Lenski's *Ecological-Evolutionary Theory*, Marvin Harris's *Cultural Materialism*, and Karl Marx's *Materialistic Determinism*, focus in this text is on human-environmental relationships. The book also explores how societies evolve from hunting and gathering societies to postindustrial societies, with technology as the catalyst for social change.

With the accumulation of surplus through the use of technology, students will see how social relationships change, in terms of power structures, political economy, and religion. Emphasis in this book is on macro-sociology, though micro aspects of society are addressed as well.

This text may seem historical in nature, but it is important for students to see and understand the development of society, and learn how cultures that once served a practical purpose are rendered redundant through technology. Questions as to why some societies are more developed than others are also discussed, along with global stratification in a world dominated by modern capitalism.

It is important to bear in mind that this book merely addresses a perspective in sociology, and should not be treated as a substitute for the original works mentioned. Needless to say, it is still a work in progress. Treat this book as a finger pointing you in the right direction. This text should open up questions for further inquiry; any controversies are meant to generate further discourse on the subject. This is the beginning of a journey, one that I hope you find enlightening and rewarding.

Recommended books

Harris, Marvin. 1974. *Cows, Pigs, Wars, and Witches: The Riddles of Culture*. New York: Vintage Books.

Harris, Marvin. 1998. *Good to Eat: Riddles of Food and Culture*. Long Grove, IL: Waveland Press.

Khaldun, Ibn. *The Muqaddimah: An Introduction to History*. Princeton, NJ: Princeton University Press.

What Is Sociology?

Person vs. Society

Are we free? Or are we subject to forces outside of us? Are we masters of our own fate, or are our fates determined by a greater force from without? These are questions posed by philosophers over the centuries. Of course, finding a simple answer to such complex questions is challenging.

To say that we are independent, we inadvertently ignore forces from without that play a role in shaping our choices. Conversely, to say that we are solely controlled by forces outside of us ignores our rational and cognitive abilities. If society does play a role in shaping who we are, how much influence does it really have? Likewise, if we are autonomous individuals, how independent are we from society?

As Americans, we consider individuality[1] a cherished value. We believe that we are masters of our own fate—that we are responsible for our own actions. This is understandable, as America is built on the culture of individualism.[2] We are taught to speak our minds, and that our opinion matters. We attribute our successes and failures to our own actions, and see ourselves as unique individuals.

To ignore social forces outside of us, however, is myopic. We cannot attribute all our individual choices as our own. After all, we use others as reference points and make decisions based on the reactions of others. As seen in the world of entertainment, something as personal as one's name is subject to change, in order to meet the demands of society.

What Is in a Name?

Nothing is more personal than one's name. Names establish our identity and provide us with a sense of who we are, as it reflects our culture and tradition. People, however, do change their names because of social forces. Can you recognize the following individuals, whose real names are listed?

1. Li Lianjie;
2. Li Zhenfan;

---

[1] Looking at the entire spectrum of human history, the concept of *individuality* is a relatively new phenomenon. We can trace the etymology of the word *community* to the 4th century A.D., but can only trace the etymology of the word *individuality* to the 18th century.

[2] The Constitution of the United States, as seen in the Bill of Rights (the first 10 Amendments), protects the rights of the individual.

Statue of Bruce Lee (1940–1973) on the Avenue of Stars in Hong Kong. **Would Bruce Lee be as successful if he had used his real name in the movies?**

3. Chan Kong San;
4. Stefani Joanne Angelina Germanotta;
5. Dana Owens.

If you answered Jet Li, Bruce Lee, Jackie Chan, Lady Gaga, and Queen Latifah, respectively, you are correct. The key question in this case is: Why do actors and actresses adopt a stage name rather than use their own?

Stage names make them more marketable, as their original names are difficult to remember and in some cases, hard to pronounce. Stage names should be simple, easy to associate with, and in the case of Asian actors and actresses, anglicized, in order to appeal to the American public.

When Arnold Schwarzenegger tried to break into the movie industry, there were concerns over his long surname and his thick Austrian accent. Fortunately, his name and accent did not pose problems, and his career was a success. The point here is simple: Something as personal as your name is subject to change according to societal demands.

Obesity

When it comes to obesity, beauty is definitely not in the eye of the beholder. Negative connotations are placed on those who are obese. As children, we make fun of our obese schoolmates, labeling them as greedy, lazy, people who lack self-discipline and control. We attribute their physical disposition to their individual behavior, failing to realize that obesity is truly a societal problem that has surfaced since the late 1960s and early 1970s (Thio, 2003).

Despite of all the information we have on obesity, society still places negative connotations on those who are "fat." Look at any fashion and health magazine, and we are bombarded with images of models with low body-fat counts and/or heavily muscled individuals with low body-fat percentages. It is clear in our popular culture that the less fat we have, the more attractive we look (Pope, Phillips, and Olivardia, 2000).

Approximately 60% of the American population fall into the obese category, and children are the highest at-risk group (Thio, 2003). With the proliferation of fast-food outlets, microwave meals, and a sedentary lifestyle (especially in front of the television and computer), it is easy to isolate the underlying causes of the problem. It is clear that lifestyle changes and food choices are by-products of market forces and technology.

There is also a correlation with obesity and socioeconomic class. More than any other socioeconomic class, the poor and the working poor tend to be obese (Thio, 2003). As in the case of obese children, the root of the problem is obvious. Go to any supermarket, fast-food outlet, or restaurant and you will find that it is cheaper to buy fattening foods than healthy ones. Food choices may not be an individual choice, but an economic necessity. It is clear that socioeconomic status can determine one's health, and for some, it is a matter of life and death.

Many of us believe that we express our individuality through the clothes we wear. Ask any teenager, and they will tell you that their clothes are an expression of themselves. As the father of a teenager, I can definitely tell you this from firsthand experience. This, however, is not the case. Contrary to what my son might tell me, fashion also shows one's connectedness with society. This is reinforced in Georg Simmel's essay *Fashion* (1904), wherein he discusses the dialectical relationship between individuality and society.

Victorian-Era Fashion. **Is fashion an expression of our individuality or conformity? Does it express our independence or connectedness with society?**

Individuals may shape their identity through the myriad of choices they have in the marketplace. Fashion, however, has social implications. It is structured according to class divisions, and is used as a means of social mobility. In American society, one can tell the income level of individuals by what they wear and which stores they patronize. This in turn has led to conspicuous consumption and waste as part of the American ethos (Veblen, 1994). As fashion is in constant flux and always changes, one can also be imprisoned by fashion trends[3] that are driven by market forces. After all, are not all the clothes we wear mass produced? If that is the case, how then can they be an expression of our individuality?

As seen from the examples given, individual choices, no matter how individual they may appear to be, are subject to social forces. People use society as a reference point and define and base their interpretations of social situations accordingly. Ironic as it may seem, the more individuated society becomes, the greater individuals rely on others[4] for their existence.

Common Sense: Learning About the Obvious

Many assume that sociology is simply common sense and take the subject matter lightly. This fallacy comes from our culture of individualistic egocentrism, where we all see the world through our own eyes and draw our conclusions accordingly. After all, we are taught since childhood to think for ourselves and that our opinion matters. But sociology is much more than common sense.

A private detective once told me that if you want to hide something effectively, hide it in plain sight. To him, people take for granted and do not pay attention to what they see and do every day. The same can be said about society. Though society is very much in our lives, we tend to take it for granted and assume that we know more than we do. Driving to work every day does not necessarily make me an expert in auto mechanics, eating in a restaurant may not make me a connoisseur, nor does visiting an aquarium make me a marine biologist. Similarly, living in society does not necessarily make one a sociologist.

In our daily interactions, we do have our "experts" on social issues. Ask anyone about a current event/social issue, and you usually get an opinion. They will have their own analysis, conclusions, and formulated hypotheses as to how they derived their opinion. When asked systematically how they came to their conclusions, many just fall by the wayside. The bottom line is simple: People see what they want to see, and draw conclusions according to their preconceived notions, ignoring social facts[5] in the process.

Experts in their respective fields study their area of specialty in unique ways. Sociologists are no exception. Sociology, as a social science, requires the scientific method in studying social situations and human relationships. As in all sciences, conclusions are based on fact and analysis based on logic and scientific methods. In any social inquiry, sociologists attempt to bridge the micro and macro aspects of society into their analysis in an attempt to provide a comprehensive explanation of the phenomenon in question. However, before going any further, it is important to define some basic sociological terms in order to establish a foundation.

Building Blocks of Sociology: Basic Terms and Definitions

Sociology, simply put, is the study of society. The word was coined by Auguste Comte in 1824 and was publicly used in his essay *Cours de Philosophie Positive*, originally published in 1838. The word is a derivation

---

[3] This is the case where individuals become "slaves" to fashion trends.

[4] We rely on others to sew our clothes, print the books we read, assemble the computer we use, cook our food at restaurants we patronize, etc.

---

[5] Social facts are social phenomena external of the individual.

of both Latin and Greek: *socios*, meaning "companion" in Latin, and *logos*, meaning "study of" in Greek.

Though the word *sociology* was coined in the 19th century, the study of society existed long before that. Philosophers such as Plato, Aristotle, and Confucius all discussed sociology long before the word was ever made. Italian scholars such as Avicenna argued that human beings are social creatures, while Muslim scholar Ibn Khaldun also discussed the mechanics of society and provided a hypothesis as to how society came about.

Society, simply defined, is a group of people, sharing similar lifestyles, who live in the same geographical region. In terms of similar lifestyles, we are referring to

Auguste Comte (1798–1857). **Comte got his foundations on positivism from Henri de Saint-Simon, under whom he served as a secretary during his youth. Comte wanted to establish sociology as a science, using scientific methods in its social inquiry.**

common institutions, cultures, and languages, where people have interdependent relationships with one another. This definition is applicable to preindustrial societies, but may seem a little archaic in a modern-day context.

We now have people of different nationalities and ethnicities, who speak different languages, living in the same geographical region. Furthermore, the idea of a common geographical region is negated by the Internet and technology. The Internet has created numerous "cyber societies," where people from all over the world can communicate and form a common bond. Perhaps we can now see ourselves as a global society.

Society is made up of various institutions. Institutions are enduring patterns of human relationships: social patterns that are passed from one generation to the next (Abercrombie, Hill, and Turner, 1994; Thio, 2003). An institution can be as small as a family and as large as the government. Institutions include, but are not limited to, the following: family, education, religion, economic system, political system, and the military.

Institutions are made up of social groups—two or more interacting[6] individuals who form a social relationship. Social groups are divided into two groups: primary and secondary groups. Primary groups[7] are small in number and have intimate relationships. Interactions, in this case, are generally informal, and the relationship is long and enduring. Secondary groups[8], on the other hand, are usually task oriented,

---

[6] Individuals, who are together, but do not interact, or interact minimally, are called a *social aggregate*. Imagine people together in an elevator or riding together in a subway, etc.

[7] Think of your relationship with your family members, close friends, and significant other, in this case.

[8] Think of the college courses you are currently enrolled in: your role is formal, and the duration of your relationship between your fellow classmates and teacher lasts for a fixed duration. Once the course is over and the grades are awarded, the relationship of this secondary group ends.

large in number, and whose relationships are formal. Relationships among group members are temporary, and once the task or objective of the groups is achieved, the group disperses (Abercrombie, Hill, and Turner, 1994; Thio, 2003).

Social groups consist of people occupying various statuses. Status is the position one holds in society. In a family, a person holds the status of father, another of mother, and others, children. Likewise, in a classroom, one holds the status of the teacher, while the others occupy the status of students. There are two types of status: ascribed status and achieved status (Abercrombie, Hill, and Turner, 1994; Thio, 2003).

Ascribed status is the status you are born into. This is best applicable in feudal systems[9] during the preindustrial age, where social mobility[10] was practically nonexistent. Ascribed status is one that you cannot get out of, and in most cases, determines your life chances. Ascribed status, in a modern context, can be one's race and sex. Achieved status, on the other hand, is the status one earns, and it is applicable in societies where social mobility and meritocracy[11] are high. In today's context, we can enhance our social mobility through education and economic success (Abercrombie, Hill, and Turner, 1994; Thio, 2003).

Every status encompasses numerous roles, specific functions in relation to one's status (Abercrombie, Hill, and Turner, 1994; Thio, 2003). A professor at a university, for example, plays the role of a teacher, an adviser, mentor, member of several committees, and a researcher. Likewise, an undergraduate can also play the role of a student, athlete, fraternity/sorority member, student worker, and friend and colleague with other undergraduates.

When the various roles pertaining to a status start to bear down and overwhelm the individual, we can say that the individual is experiencing a role strain (Abercrombie, Hill, and Turner, 1994; Thio, 2003). A married, practicing attorney with children may find balancing the different roles of a husband to his wife, father to his children, and a lawyer to his clients overwhelming. Likewise, an undergraduate may find it challenging to balance the role of student, athlete, friend, and fraternity/sorority member.

There are times when the different roles pertaining to the same status come in opposition with one another. When this occurs, we call this a role conflict (Abercrombie, Hill, and Turner, 1994; Thio, 2003). A student, for example, may have to sacrifice one role over another when the situation demands it. Due to a big exam, a student may have to forgo an important student government meeting so she can study. Likewise, a professor may have to relinquish some of her teaching duties in order to have an article published.

Statuses and roles play an important part in society, as they establish one's relationship in regard to others (Abercrombie, Hill, and Turner, 1994; Thio, 2003). Status and roles may seem complicated in a modern-day context, but, as in every aspect of society, they go through an evolutionary process, as further discussion in later sections of the book will illustrate. You will learn that institutions, status, and roles play an important part in holding society together, by ensuring its continuity for generations to come, and how they evolve through time with technology as the catalyst for social change. Although institutions, social groups, status, and roles define social relationships, social relationships are held together by culture,[12] ways of life that characterize a society. There are three elements of culture: beliefs, values, and norms (Abercrombie, Hill, and Turner, 1994; Thio, 2003).

Beliefs, simply put, are definitions that are assumed to be true (Abercrombie, Hill, and Turner, 1994; Thio, 2003). The key word here is *assumed*.

---

[9] Good examples of this are royalty, nobility, and the aristocracy. The practical purpose of ascribed statuses is to keep wealth within a limited social circle.

[10] Social mobility is the ability to move from one level of society to the next.

[11] This is based on one's merit and ability.

[12] It is important to note that cultures serve a practical purpose, usually tied to the human-environmental relationship of respective societies.

There is no empirical[13] proof as to why the assumption is made, but it is made nevertheless. Some people believe in the existence of God, though there is no empirical proof. Nevertheless, the belief is there, and one's thoughts and actions are shaped according to one's beliefs.

Values are social agreements on what is good, bad, desirable, and undesirable (Abercrombie, Hill, and Turner, 1994; Thio, 2003). Hindus, for example, see the cow as a sacred animal, and the animal is thus venerated. Hence, eating beef is considered bad. Muslims, on the other hand, consider the pig an unclean animal, and so eating pork is bad. How these two religions have such contrasting values is another point of discussion reserved for later sections of the book. It is important to note that values play an important part toward one's understanding of the world, and how social situations are interpreted and acted upon.

Norms are rules for behavior, how one should or should not act in social situations. There are three types of norms: folkways, mores, and laws. Folkways are the customs and manners of a society (Abercrombie, Hill, and Turner, 1994; Thio, 2003). When someone stretches out his or her hand, you reciprocate likewise, and shake hands. Thais do the customary "Wai" when they greet one another, while the Japanese bow[14] when greeting someone. Likewise, it is customary in most Asian cultures to venerate the elderly and to take off one's shoes upon entering the home of another. When one violates folkways, one is considered rude or uncouth by other members of society. However, violating folkways may not necessarily violate mores or laws[15] (Abercrombie, Hill, and Turner, 1994; Thio, 2003).

Mores (pronounced *morays*[16]) are based on the moral standards of the society. Mores are usually backed by religion, which ensures its continuity for future generations. Mores help maintain social order, but not all mores are backed by law (Abercrombie, Hill, and Turner, 1994; Thio, 2003). In the Judeo-Christian tradition, it is morally wrong to commit adultery, though it is not illegal in the United States. On the same note, murder is both illegal and morally wrong. Thus, laws are formalized and backed by society. Violation of laws can lead to sanctions,[17] some of which may be severe, depending on the crime committed (Abercrombie, Hill, and Turner, 1994; Thio, 2003).

As mentioned earlier, culture defines our social relationships by shaping our definitions of our situations, and acts as a guide during times of uncertainty. Culture permeates every aspect of our lives: through our institutions, social groups, roles, and statuses. In many ways, culture becomes the bonding agent that holds society together, providing people with an identity, sense of belonging, and self. Figure 1.1 summarizes the building blocks of society and how they are connected and held together. Definitions of the terms used are also provided to give you a better understanding of the subject matter.

---

[13] The word comes from a philosophical thought that originated in Great Britain. British empiricists such as John Locke, believed that knowledge is acquired through sensory input: hence, what is assumed true, must be touched seen, smelled, etc.

[14] The height of the bow (high or low) demarcates the person's social status in relation to the other.

---

[15] Being rude is not necessarily immoral or illegal.

[16] Just think of moray eels.

[17] These are the consequences we face for violating customs, laws, etc.

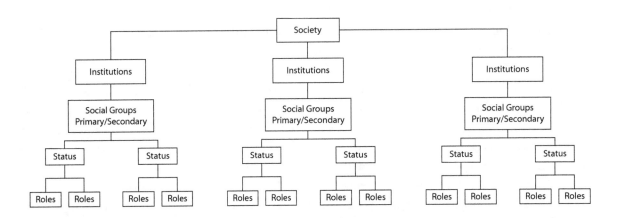

Figure 1.1: Breakdown of Society into Institutions, Statuses, and Roles

1. Societies are made up of several Institutions: *enduring patterns of human relationships.*
2. Institutions are made up of Social Groups: *two or more interacting individuals, who form a social relationship.*
3. Social Groups consist of individuals holding various Statuses: *the position one holds in relation to one's social group.*
4. Each Status encompasses numerous roles.
5. Institutions, Statuses, and Roles define our relationships with one another.
6. Society and social relationships are also defined according to Norms, Values, Cultures, and Customs.

The Origins of Society

Theories on the Evolution of Societies

We do not exactly know how societies originated, although scholars throughout history have put forth their respective hypotheses. Three major scholars are mentioned in this chapter who have contributed immensely to the field. These three have relatively similar ideas, with variations that are reflected in the intellectual discourse of their respective eras. The scholars are as follows:

Ibn Khaldun (1332–1406)

The fourteenth-century Muslim scholar Ibn Khaldun wrote a book called *The Muqaddimah* (originally published in 1370). In it, he argues that humans, left to their own devices, are helpless creatures compared to creatures having the natural disposition to hunt. Humans, however, have three attributes that put them above other creatures: their ability to think, the use of their hands, and their ability to cooperate for mutual benefit.

Consistent with the philosophy of Ibn Sina, otherwise known by his Latin name Avicenna (980 A.D.–1037 A.D.), Khaldun argued that humans are social creatures. It is important to note that Khaldun never saw cooperation as altruistic in nature. Humans are naturally selfish, and cooperation was merely a

Ibn Khaldun (1332–1406).

necessary means to an end: self-preservation. Khaldun believed that royal authority was natural for humans. Humans have a natural inclination to follow royal authority, and it takes a benevolent leader to keep order in society through group solidarity, or "group feelings."

Reading *The Muqaddimah* (1967) provides insights into how Muslim societies operated during the Golden Age of Islam. The Muslims during Khaldun's time were technologically more advanced compared with their European counterparts. Europe was slowly coming out of the Dark Ages, and the Muslims were already experimenting with physics, chemistry, and astronomy. It was not until the Renaissance that the Europeans reached their "takeoff" point. They eventually bypassed Islamic civilization during the Industrial Revolution.

Thomas Hobbes (1588–1679)

In his treatise *Leviathan* (originally published in 1651), Hobbes displayed similar sentiments. Like Khaldun, Hobbes argued that human are selfish, self-serving creatures, who seek two major objectives: self-preservation and power. In order to ensure self-preservation and to keep the selfish impulses of others in check, humans enter into a social contract and surrender all independence and authority to a single ruler. It is through the social contract where one shares a "Commonwealth," and society, in itself, becomes a "Leviathan."

In the image published in Hobbes's original work, we see the image of a man with a crown, symbolizing royal authority, wielding a sword—the symbol of a protector. Note that his body is made up of numerous individuals,

Image appearing on the cover of
***Leviathan* in 1651.**

symbolizing society. Hence, it is through society that one enters a social contract and surrenders one's freedom to a ruler who protects the welfare of the masses.

Jean-Jacques Rousseau (1712–1778)

Rousseau provides a different perspective on the social contract theory. While it is true that people should enter into a contract for self-preservation, they should, however, be given the opportunity to reach a consensus as to what rules to live by—and when necessary, have the ability to revise the laws as needed. Unlike Khaldun and Hobbes,

Jean-Jacques Rousseau (1712–1778).

who believed in a sovereign, Rousseau leaned toward popular sovereignty, or "general will."

Discussion of the various political and governmental systems is reserved for later chapters when you will learn how a sovereign rules, and that the political economy behind each social system is tied to human-environmental relationships.

The Evolution of Societies: Respective Theories

Societies, like all living organisms, evolve from one stage to the next. Key questions concerning the evolutionary theory are: How do societies evolve from one stage to the next, and why are some societies more evolved or advanced compared to others? Furthermore, what is the major catalyst for social change? This section explores several explanations put forth by various social thinkers and provides a theoretical perspective that this discussion follows.

Herbert Spencer

History has been hard on Herbert Spencer, the English sociologist who coined the phrase "survival of the fittest."[1] Modeled out of Charles Darwin's theory of evolution, Spencer applied Darwin's theory to society. In order to get a better understanding of Spencer's theory, it is important to provide some background information on Darwin's theory of evolution (Spencer, 1971).

Darwin,[2] in his study of organisms while sailing on the HMS *Beagle* in the Galapagos Islands, asked a simple question: Why are some species able to evolve and survive, while others become extinct? To provide an explanation, Darwin came up with the term "natural selection"—the ability of organisms to adapt to the changes in their environment. Darwin's hypothesis was simple: Species that are best able to adapt to changes in their

Herbert Spencer (1820–1903) at age 38.

respective environments evolve, while those that cannot adapt become extinct.

Spencer developed his theory on the evolution of societies based on Darwin's natural selection model. Spencer argued that societies go through stages of evolution—developing from simple, undifferentiated[3] societies to complex, differentiated ones. Societies, according to Spencer, go through four main societal stages: Simple, Compound, Doubly Compound, and Trebly Compound (Spencer, 1971).

Simple societies are societies with no formal or rudimentary forms of political relationships. Hunting and gathering tribes such as the Pueblos, Australian aborigines, and the Karen people from Burma are some examples. Simple societies vary from *Headless*[4] to tribes with *Stable Headships*,[5] but the differentiation is low compared to other societal types (Spencer, 1971).

Compound societies have forms of formal leadership, centralized government, social rankings,[6] and more advanced forms of division of labor. The bedouins, fifth-century Teutons, and ancient Yucatan are some examples of compound societies. Greater

---

[1] The phrase "survival of the fittest" has often been mistakenly associated with Charles Darwin. Nowhere in Darwin's *Origins of Species*, originally published in 1859, was this phrase "survival of the fittest" ever found.

[2] Charles Darwin was an ordained Anglican minister. Before taking charge of a parish, he decided to tour the world on the H.M.S. *Beagle*. His major role was to be the ship captain's "dinner mate", while at sea. Darwin had an interest in the natural sciences as a little boy, and this interest was enhanced while at sea.

[3] Spencer saw differentiation in forms of social classes, religion, political organizations, and social stratification (different levels in society). The more differentiated a society is, the greater the advancement.

[4] Tribes with no leaders.

[5] These are tribes with a head; this is consistent over a long duration.

[6] Spencer mentioned social rankings divided into five or six different levels.

differentiations are seen in Doubly Compound societies through more complex governments and technological advancements (Spencer, 1971).

One notable fact Spencer mentioned that separate Doubly Compound Societies from Compound Societies is the fact that they all live in permanent settlements. Spencer also mentioned the presence of a "developed ecclesiastical[7] hierarchy," along with industrial organizations based on the caste system. Customs are passed into laws at this stage, and religions have become institutionalized. Towns and roads are established, and development of arts and sciences are present (Spencer, 1971).

Charles Darwin (1809–1882). **Portrait of a young Charles Darwin.**

According to Spencer, civilizations such as ancient Mexico, the Assyrian and Egyptian empires, the Roman Empire, modern Great Britain, France, Germany, Italy, and Russia are examples of Trebly Compound Societies. These are civilizations that are the most advanced and differentiated of all (Spencer, 1971).

How, then, does one civilization evolve from one stage to the next? Spencer's Military Phase Model provides an explanation.

According to the Military Phase Model, Spencer believes that all civilizations begin at the Barbarian stage. It is at the Barbarian stage where humans cooperate with the premise of self-preservation; competition with other tribes makes it necessary to fight. It is through the act of war that civilizations are forced to evolve to the Militant Phase, a phase where societies are organized on survival (Spencer, 1971).

Technology at the Military Phase focuses on military weapons—survival is based on warfare. There is little room for individuality, and allegiance is to the tribe and community. Natural leaders[8] are those who are able to hold the populace together and lead the troops into battle. The major premise here is to conquer and expand one's civilization (Spencer, 1971).

However, every society at the military phase has its limitations, and can only conquer so much. Once opposing tribes are subjugated and the need for war is negated, societies at this stage arrive at the state of Equilibration. This is the stage where the society departs from their martial technological innovations and focuses on science and technology.[9] It is through this stage that the society evolves into the Industrial Stage (Spencer, 1971).

---

[7] An assembly of citizens or an established institution.

[8] A good example of societies in the Military Phase is the Mongol Empire under the leadership of Genghis Khan.

[9] This is best illustrated through the Golden Age of Islam (7th to 15th centuries A.D.), and the Pax Romana (96 to 180 A.D.).

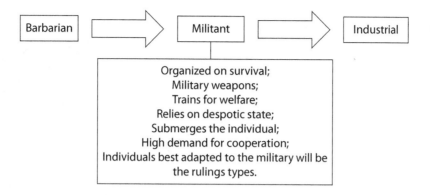

The power to adapt is based on three premises:

1. Innovation;
2. Technology;
3. General will to survive.

Figure 2.1. Herbert Spencer's Military Phase Model

Spencer believes that the survival of societies lies in their power to adapt, and this power to adapt rests on three basic principles: innovation, technology, and the general will to survive. Hence, the societies that are best able to adapt, survive and evolve. Those less able to do so are subjugated or go extinct (Spencer, 1971).

Spencer's theory of societal evolution was very popular during his time. After all, Great Britain was at its zenith of power, and his theory provided legitimization for Britain's colonizing countries in Asia, Africa, and the Americas. Over time, the theory started losing popularity, and Spencer's contribution to sociology is largely forgotten or dismissed.[10] Looking back in retrospect, one must credit Spencer for his attempts in providing a theoretical perspective on the evolution of societies. Though many may not embrace his social Darwinism perspective, he does see technology as the catalyst for change—a view shared by Karl Marx.

Karl Marx: Materialistic Determinism

Like Spencer, Karl Marx saw technological advances as the catalyst for social change. Unlike most thinkers of his time, Marx was a materialistic determinist, paying attention to the material conceptions of life. Unlike Georg Wilhelm Friedrich Hegel, who felt that it was ideas that shaped material conditions, Marx believed that it was the other way around: material conditions shaped a person's perception of reality.[11]

In his analysis of societies, Marx paid attention to the means of production. He divided societies into two major components: the Infrastructure and the Superstructure. The Infrastructure serves as the mode of production—the base of operation, consisting of the Forces of Production (technology, raw materials, natural resources, and machines), and the Relations to Production (ownership of the Means of Production). The Superstructure, on the other hand, deals with the cultural ideals and values (of the society in question).

According to Marx, the Infrastructure and the Superstructure are directly related. Changes in the Infrastructure through technology would lead to

---

[10] It is interesting to note that Herbert Spencer's grave is directly opposite Karl Marx's in Highgate Cemetery in London, England. Marx's grave is treated as a shrine, while Spencer's grave is largely ignored.

[11] This was where Marx successfully turned Hegel's theory "on its head".

changes in the Superstructure. The direct causation that leads to changes in human thoughts and ideas comes from the Infrastructure, and not the other way around. Changes come when there is a contradiction in the Infrastructure, and this is where society evolves from one stage to the next (Sanderson and Alderson, 2005), as the following illustrates:

Simple societies practice Primitive Communism. Good examples of these are hunting and gathering and pastoral societies. Simple tools like bows, arrows, and digging sticks are used for hunting and simple agriculture. Greater innovations, like the use of digging hoes, lead to greater accumulation of surplus, which inevitably leads to contradictions to the existing status quo—there are those who control the means of production, while others do not. This leads to a contradiction between the Infrastructure and Superstructure. With this contradiction, society evolves to the next stage (Sanderson and Alderson, 2005).

Marx called slavery the Ancient Mode of Production. Ancient Egypt and ancient Rome are examples of this. Slaves engage in the production process, while their masters own the means of production. Slavery is most effective in warlike societies, where jobs are labor intensive and conquests and occupations are common. However, when the stage of equilibration[12] is reached, slavery[13] can be expensive. Contradictions in slavery lead to the evolution to the next stage—the Feudal Mode of Production (Sanderson and Alderson, 2005).

The Feudal Mode of Production is most effective in agrarian societies. With the use of fertilizers and the horse-drawn plow, farmers can produce food at a much quicker rate. With greater accumulation of surplus, stratification is greatest here. There are nobility, landowners, tenant farmers, and serfs. Medieval Europe is the best example of the Feudal Mode of

Karl Marx (1818–1883). **Portrait of Karl Marx as a teenager.**

Production. Contradictions to the feudal system began during the Renaissance period and were evident during the advent of the Industrial Revolution (Sanderson and Alderson, 2005).

With the mass production of consumer goods and mass consumption during the Industrial Age, capitalism became the economic model. Marx spent his entire life trying to educate people on the evils of capitalism. He felt that contradictions in the oppressive system would eventually lead to a change, with the replacement of capitalism by socialism. As mentioned earlier, Marx saw technology as the catalyst for social

---

[12] Term borrowed from Herbert Spencer.

[13] One has to feed one's slaves, and tend to them when they are ill. This becomes expensive when the costs outweighs the profits.

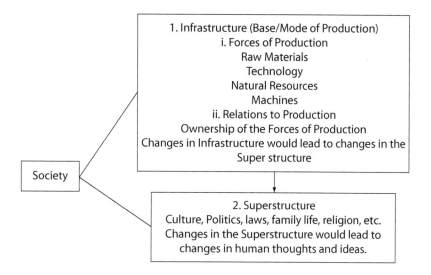

Figure 2.2. Karl Marx's Two Major Societal Components

Figure 2.3. Karl Marx's Stages of Societal Evolution

change, but his emphasis was strictly on the means of production and the effects it has on society in general.

Marvin Harris: Cultural Materialism

Though an anthropologist, Marvin Harris's contribution to the field of sociology is invaluable. Modeled on the orthodox Marxian model, Harris's Cultural Materialism[14] theory takes into consideration the environment, ecology and population density, sex ratio, and growth rates. Unlike Marx, Harris stresses the human-environmental relationships of societies and

how they maintain a symbiotic connection. Primitive cultures, according to Harris, serve practical purposes, in that they help preserve the environment—in turn, the environment ensures the survival of the community by maintaining Ecological Equilibrium.[15] Harris divides societies into three components (Sanderson and Alderson, 2005), as Figure 2.4 illustrates:

For Harris, evolution starts from the Infrastructure, which subsequently sets off changes in both the Structure and Infrastructure. Attention is paid to the intensification of production and environmental depletion.[16] This is due to population growth, resulting

---

[14] Those who are familiar with Karl Marx would argue that Harris was a neo-Marxist. His Cultural Materialism Model is relatively similar to Marx's Materialistic Determinism. Unlike Marx, however, Harris does not pay sole attention to the Means of Production.

[15] This is best explained in Marvin Harris's *Cows, Pigs, Wars, and Witches* (1974).

[16] Every environment has a limited Carrying Capacity: the ability of the environment to sustain itself and the organisms that live within it.

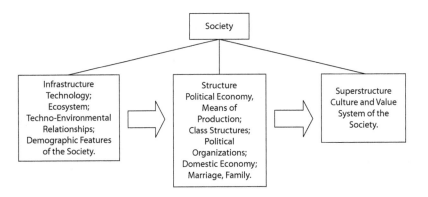

Figure 2.4. Cultural Materialism: Three Components of Society

in the increase of Population Pressure,[17] which in turn requires the intensification of production. Population growth is the key component to the evolution of society from one stage to the next.

Marvin Harris (1927–2001).

As the population grows, the more people have to work to keep up with the increase. With the greater demand for food, people are forced to look for ways to produce food at a much faster rate, resulting in innovation and technology. With technological advances, societies evolve from one stage to the next.

Gerhard Lenski

Gerhard Lenski's Ecological-Evolutionary Theory stresses food-producing technology as the catalyst for social change. Greater use of the environment through technological advances results in population growth. With greater control of the food production process, societies are able to settle in permanent settlements. In line with the Marxian model, greater technological advancements lead to greater accumulation of surplus, which in turn leads to greater social differentiation and occupational specialization. According to Lenski's model, societies are classed according to their food-production technology and the stage of Ecological Evolution achieved (Lenski, 2005; Sanderson and Alderson, 2005).

Social-Cultural Evolution Theory

In order to bring together all the theories mentioned, this text adopts a syncretism of approaches mentioned, which I will call the *Social-Cultural Evolution Theory*. We attempt to address the weaknesses and enhance the strengths of each theorist, giving the reader a better understanding of the evolution of societies.

Following Harris's Cultural Materialism, attention is given to the human-environmental

---

[17] This is the pressure the population exerts on the Carrying Capacity of the environment: the greater the population, the greater the Population Pressure. Hence, the greater the Population Pressure, the greater strain it has on the environment.

relationship. Environment shapes cultures. Cultures, in turn, serve to preserve the environment. In order to preserve the practices of previous generations for future generations, religion intercedes to ensure continuity. Hence, religion preserves both environment and culture—while at the same time, culture and environment serve to preserve the environment. Consistent with Herbert Spencer's Societal Evolution Model, civilizations that are most able to adapt and maximize their environmental disposition are the ones most likely to survive.

In simple societies, environment, culture, and religion shapes the political economy[18] of the society. The Redistributive Forces/Market System, in turn, determines the type of government, and the type of government shapes the type of society. Finally, the type of society inadvertently shapes the cultural ideation[19] of the individual.

At the same time, the type of government reinforces the existing Redistributive Forces/Market System, which is legitimized by the existing cultural and religious values, whose practical objective is to preserve the environment.

Consistent with the theoretical perspectives of Spencer, Marx, Harris, and Lenski, technology[20] serves as the catalyst for social change. Technology, in general, remains as the independent variable,[21] though the type of government[22] can influence the type of technology considered valuable, as in the case of the Soviet Union during the Cold War (1945–1989).

Gerhard Lenski (1924–Present).

Technological advancements, especially through the means of production, change the Redistributive Forces/Market System of the society in question.[23] This subsequently changes the cultural and religious values of the society in question, and the human-environmental relationships.[24] Likewise, changes in the Redistributive Forces/Market System bring changes in the type of government, which influence the societal type, which inevitably influences the cultural ideation of individuals.

In the following chapters, discussion on the various types of societies will bring this theoretical perspective to light. Careful attention is given to the

---

[18] How goods and services are produced, managed, and distributed among the population.

[19] Idea generation.

[20] Unlike Lenski, who focuses solely on food- producing technology, this theoretical perspective looks at technology in general.

[21] The variable that remains unchanged.

[22] This was the time that the Soviet Union invested heavily in the Military Industrial Complex: (as seen in the perforated line connecting the Type of Government and Technology in Figure 1.5).

---

[23] This is best illustrated through the Industrial Revolution, where mass production and consumption, saw the rise of merchants and traders through capitalism, and the demise of the feudal system and aristocracys.

[24] Discussion on the Renaissance, Industrial Revolution, and Protestant Reformation, in later sections of this book, will illustrate the point further.

human-environmental relationships and how technology acts as a catalyst for social change, bringing out the evolution of societies from one stage to the next.

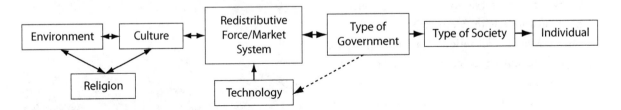

1. Environment shapes cultures.
2. Cultures, in turn, help to preserve the environment.
3. Religions are shaped by both environment and culture. This in turn preserves environment and culture by ensuring the continuation of norms, customs, and values.
4. Environments, cultures, and religions help shape and reinforce the Redistributive Forces/Market System.
5. The Redistributive Forces/Market System in turn reinforces the existing cultures, religion, and environment.
6. The Redistributive Forces/Market System determines the type of government.
7. The type of government determines the type of society.
8. Technology,[1] through the changes in the means of production, changes the Redistributive Forces/Market System of the society.
9. Changes in the Redistributive Forces/Market System take a two-pronged attack: to the left, changes in culture, religion, and the environment; to the right, changes in the type of government and the type of society.
10. The type of society influences individual behavior, values, preferences, and wants.

It is important to understand that technology is the catalyst for social change. Unlike Lenski, who focuses on food-production technology, this theoretical perspective encompasses all technology.

Figure 2.5. Social-Cultural Evolution Theory[2]

---

[1] Technology, in most cases, remains the Independent Variable. Though as seen in the Soviet Union, the type of government influenced which technological advances were most relevant—in this case, the Military Industrial Complex. Hence, we see the perforated line connecting the Type of Government with Technology.

[2] This theoretical perspective is modeled on Gerhard Lenski's Ecological-Evolutionary Theory, Marvin Harris's Cultural Materialism, Karl Marx's Materialistic Determinism, Emile Durkheim's Communalism, Max Weber's Bureaucratic Rationalization, and Symbolic Interaction.

Research Methods

Conducting Social Research

Since sociology is a science, it requires a scientific methodology in the process of gathering data. Theories are merely propositions, and one must also acquire empirical evidence to prove or disprove one's proposition. Hence, it is important to understand the various research methods used by social scientists and how they gather data relevant to their study in question.

Discussion will cover the stages in conducting research, the various research methods, and the best methods used in relation to one's research question and hypothesis. Also included in this chapter are ethical issues pertaining to social research and the various steps social scientists should take in order to protect their study participants.

Stages of Conducting Research

Step One: Formulate a Research Question

As in any first step of any social research, this is the stage where the researcher finds a topic of interest, focusing on areas that might provide interesting insights and questions. Topics such as race, class, gender, immigration, crime, etc. make for interesting research questions, as they are multifaceted areas that can generate all kinds of discussion. For the sake of discussion, we will use the research question of religiosity (how religious people are) in our search for the right research method. With religiosity in mind, it would be interesting to find out how religious people are, and what pertains to being religious.

Step Two: Review of the Literature

This is an important step, as it is important to gather as much background information on the subject as possible before embarking on the project. This is where the researcher goes to the library to check books, articles, and past studies on the subject matter and discovers what past research has uncovered, as well as any problems encountered in the process. One can learn about weaknesses of past studies and avoid potential pitfalls that might come along the way. Reviewing the literature on the subject matter is also another way of seeing if the research question is suitable, given the circumstances[1] one has.

---

[1] One must take into consideration the resources one has, such as time and money.

Step Three: Define Variables in Question

Variables must be events, features, or characteristics that are subject to change. More importantly, variables must be measurable—otherwise, the study may not work. In the case of our study on religiosity, variables that come to mind are as follows:

i. Prayer;
ii. Reading the Bible;
iii. Church Services;
iv. Church Participation;
v. Church Donations.

Each of the above mentioned variables is measurable, as the next stage illustrates.

Step Four: Operationally Define Variables

When we say "operationally define" a variable, we are simply stating how a variable is to be measured (Babbie, 1990; Schutt, 2006). As seen in the variables mentioned in the previous stage, we can operationally define the variable Prayer by the number of times one prays a day and the average duration each time. Likewise, we can operationally define Reading the Bible as the number of times one reads the Bible each day and the length of each session, etc. After all the variables are operationally defined, it is time to move on to the next stage.

Step Five: Form a Hypothesis

Simply put, a hypothesis is an inference, prediction, or educated guess as to how variables are related to one another (Schutt, 2006). For example, one can make an educated guess that the more sugar you give a child, the more likely he or she is going to be hyperactive. Likewise, it is logical to conclude that the more one studies, the greater the likelihood that one is going to do well on an exam. As seen from the examples, these are merely calculated guesses. In the case of our study on religiosity, the following hypothesis can be made:

Students from a private Christian religious university are more religious compared to Christian students from a public, secular university.

On the surface, this inference seems logical. The task now is to prove or disprove it. In order to do so, one must choose the research method that best fits the hypothesis in question.

Step Six: Data Gathering

The process of gathering data depends on the research method employed. The research method used is contingent on the research question and hypothesis. Discussion of the various research methods employed by social scientists is reserved for the following section.

Step Seven: Data Analysis

Data analysis occurs after all relevant information is gathered. Contingent on the type of research method used, analysis can be quantitative, where statistical methods such as frequencies (mean, median, and mode) and correlations (the relationship between the variables studied) are used; or qualitative, where the researcher looks for themes that develop from their respective social settings gathered through nonparticipant or participant observations.

Step Eight: Write the Report

Once data analysis is completed, the researcher writes a report on the study. In the report, the researcher will relate whether the findings support or do not support the hypothesis, or that more information should be gathered before reaching a definitive answer. It is important to note that an inconclusive result does not necessarily mean an inferior research. This may be an indication that other variables may come into play, or that other dimensions of human behavior should also be explored. The study may also open up new research

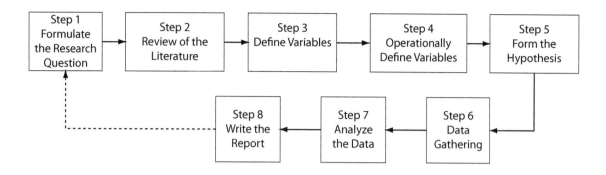

Figure 3.1 Linear Sequence of Social Research

Steps 8 to 1

Sometimes the result of a research generates new research questions, and this in turn leads to a new research altogether. With new research at hand, one returns to Step 1 and repeats the process again

Terms and Definitions

Hypothesis:	Educated guess as to how one variable is related to another.
Population:	Entire group of people being studied.
Sample:	Small number of people selected from the population to study.
Variable:	Events, features, and characteristics that are subject to change.
Reliability:	Can someone else replicate your study?
Validity:	Are you measuring what you are supposed to measure?
Experimental Designs:	Used when you are interested in studying "cause" and "effect" between variables.
Independent Variable:	The variable that remains unchanged (the stimulant in Experimental Designs).
Dependent Variable:	The variable that changes.
Control Group:	The group that does not receive the "stimulant" in Experimental Designs.
Experimental Group:	The group that receives the "stimulant" in Experimental Designs.
Survey Research Methods:	Administer surveys or questionnaires, or interview participants directly. Used when you want to get to the largest number of people over the shortest period of time. Ideal when financial and time budgets are tight. Survey Research Methods can be Qualitative or Quantitative.
Open-Ended Questions:	Questions that allow participants to respond in their own words.
Closed-Ended Questions:	Questions that do not allow participants to respond in their own words. Participants in the case are

Types of Sampling

Random Sampling:	Throw names in a hat and pull names out systematically. Select participants randomly without a system.
Systematic Sampling:	Involves a type of system like selecting every third person in the telephone book for an interview.
Snowball Sampling:	Think of a snowball rolling down a hill—it gets bigger as it goes along. After interviewing one participant, you ask him or her to refer you to three people he or she knows, who are willing to participate. You then repeat the process again by asking the three you interviewed to refer you to three more.
Stratified Sampling:	Population divided into units (males/females, urban/suburban, etc); drawing a random sample where various segments of the population are represented in proportion, reflecting that of the population.
Qualitative Research Methods:	Research methods based on observation; not based on quantitative measurements and precise claims. Qualitative Research Methods are best used when researchers are interested in understanding the subjective realities of the people being studied.
Nonparticipant Observation:	This is where the researcher remains unobtrusive and observes at a distance. This is done in order to avoid the Hawthorne Effect, where people's behavior change when they know they are being observed.
Participant Observation:	This is where the researcher participates in the daily activities of the population. They participate in their ceremonies, rituals, and day-to-day activities in order to derive an understanding of the subjective realities of the population studied.
Secondary Data Research:	Use of existing data to do research. Content Analysis would fall under this category.

questions, which may lead to further research in the future.

Types of Research Methods

Taking into consideration our research question on religiosity, we will explore the various research methods used by social scientists. Studying the characteristics and features of each research method, we will select the research method that is most suitable in gathering the data that best answers our research question and hypothesis.

Content Analysis

This is the process where researchers codify and analyze documents like newspapers, magazines, and fiction novels with the purpose of explaining and describing themes pertaining to a social phenomenon. For example, one who is interested in studying gender issues may look out for the language used to describe women and men, their respective portrayals in novels, pictures depicting men and women in advertisements, magazines, etc. It is based on these observations that one threads developing themes and common denominators. Erving Goffman's *Gender*

***Rory Leidelmeyer (1994), Mr. Universe WBF 1989.* Which research method would we use if we wanted to see the effects of creatine monohydrate on muscle mass and strength?**

Advertisements (1976) is a good example of Content Analysis. Looking at our research question on religiosity, it is clear that Content Analysis is not the correct research method to use, as it does not address our operational definitions of the variables we want to study.

Experimental Designs

Experimental Designs are conducted in a controlled setting such as a laboratory, where other intervening variables are controlled. This is to ensure that the relationship between the two variables studied is not spurious.[2] Experimental Designs are best used for studying "cause" and "effect," where the Independent Variable (the variable that remains unchanged) is manipulated to see if there is an effect on the Dependent Variable (the variable that is subject to change and being studied).

Experimental Designs are ideal when you want to test the effects of sugar on the hyperactivity of children or the effects of creatine monohydrate[3] on strength performance. In terms of sugar and hyperactivity, one can see if there is a correlation between the number of doses of sugar and the duration of hyperactive activities displayed by the child. On that same note, one can also see if there is a correlation between the number of doses of creatine monohydrate and the percentage increase in strength and muscle mass of the athlete.

Correlation is found through the Correlation Coefficient[4] which falls from the -1 to 1 range. The negative (-) sign would mean a negative relationship (the more spoonfuls of sugar, the less hyperactive the child), and the positive sign (+) would mean a positive relationship (the more spoonfuls of sugar, the more hyperactive the child). The relationship is significant at the .5 and above level.

Experimental Designs are best when you are looking for causal relationships. It can, however, be time consuming and expensive, as the experiments have to be conducted in a laboratory setting. Thus, this research method is not suitable if you have strict financial and time budgets. Since the study is conducted in a laboratory setting, it is difficult to have a large sample size; the results cannot be generalized to the general population in their natural settings.

Experimental Designs are rarely used by sociologists, though social psychologists do use features of Experimental Designs to test their hypotheses. Taking

---

[2] The relationship between the two variables studied is actually caused by a third.

[3] This is an amino acid used by bodybuilders. It is sold by supplement outlets.

[4] This is derived through a statistical method.

into consideration our study on religiosity, our hypothesis does not call for a causal relationship. Hence, Experimental Designs are not suitable for our research in question.

Secondary Data Research

When it comes to cost effectiveness, Secondary Data Research is the least expensive. This is where you gather information through existing documents such as books, articles, and periodicals. The main advantage of Secondary Data Research is that the information is readily accessible, which saves time and money. There is no need to interview others or send out surveys, which can be costly and time consuming.

In the case of our study on religiosity, we can look up past studies on the topic, and see what conclusions others drew on the subject. However, one is also limited to data that already exists, and as unfortunate as this may seem, there is a possibility that one may not be able to find any existing data that is relevant to the research in question. Furthermore, information gathered may be dated, and attitudes toward religiosity may have changed over time. We cannot generalize religious attitudes of people 20 years ago to the population today, as attitudes, cultures, and sociopolitical climates may have changed over the years. Thus, in the case of our proposed study, Secondary Data Collection may be helpful, but it may not be the best method possible in relation to our research question and hypothesis.

Secondary Data Research is best for research topics that cover populations of the past. For example, if you wish to study the lives of women during the Middle Ages, history books, articles, and periodicals are excellent resources. Other research methods would not be viable, as the participants are no longer with us.

Field Research (Qualitative Research)

Field Research falls under the category of Qualitative Research Methods, as researchers are interested in understanding the subjective realities of the participants in question. Researchers, employing this method, generally pay attention to rituals, norms, customs, values, and behaviors of the participants, and how they understand and interpret the social world that they live in. Discussion will cover three[5] types of Field Research: Nonparticipant Observation, Participant Observation, and Case Studies.

Nonparticipant Observation

In this case, one studies social settings and group dynamics at a distance, without intruding (Lofland and Lofland, 1995; Creswell, 1998). One can study the group dynamics of people at a traffic light, train station, shopping mall, or children playing in a park by observing from a distance. It is important that one remains unobtrusive in order to avoid the Hawthorne Effect.[6] Taking detailed field notes is important, as themes may develop. For example, a person observing the group dynamics of people at a local gym may notice the following themes: the weights men lift increase approximately 10% more when women are around; and men grunt louder with women training partners, etc.

Nonparticipation Observation has its limitations when it comes to our study in religiosity. We can observe how people pray in church, recite Bible phrases, etc., but the information gathered is limited. It is clear that other variables account for religiosity, which Nonparticipant Observation is unable provide. Furthermore, the sample size is limited, and we cannot generalize the findings to the entire population (Spradley, 1980; Schutt, 2006).

---

[5] John Creswell (1998) mentions five traditions in Qualitative Research: Biography, Phenomenology, Grounded Theory, Ethnography, and Case Study. For the sake of brevity, the three methods mentioned will fall under the categories of Biography, Ethnography, and Case Study.

[6] This is an effect where people's behavior change when they know they are being observed.

Participant Observation

This is where the researcher immerses him or herself into the setting. The researcher participates in the rituals, ceremonies, and customs of the group in question, and behaves like members of the same group. It is through the interaction with the group members that one gains an understanding of the subjective realities of the group members, by seeing the world through their eyes. This research method is widely used among anthropologists studying simple societies (Creswell, 1998).

In order for Participant Observation to be really effective, one must be unobtrusive—otherwise the Hawthorne Effect may result. It is important to be able to blend into the social setting, as some cultures may be skeptical of outsiders and modify their behavior accordingly (Creswell, 1998).

Participation Observation is time consuming, and there is a propensity for one to go "native."[7] Hence, researcher's bias may occur, and this takes away any objectivity in the study. Needless to say, it can also be dangerous, especially for those studying cultures of gangs and secret societies (Lofland and Lofland, 1993; Creswell, 1998).

As mentioned, Participation Observation is time consuming and requires one to be immersed in the social setting. In terms of our study on religiosity, this method may not be the best, as the sample size is limited, and it is difficult to generalize the findings to the entire population (though we may gain valuable insights on religious rituals, festivals, and ceremonies).

Case Studies

Case Studies are best employed when the study involves an individual, group, or a specific event. Case Studies are effective when studying the life and times of individuals. Those studying the homeless may gain valuable insights of a day in the life of a homeless person through interviews. One may understand the subculture of the homeless, major events of the day, and the circumstances as to how the person became homeless. One can also gain personal experience by spending the day with the person in question, to gain a firsthand experience (Creswell, 1998).

Studying group dynamics is another area where Case Studies are effective. One can immerse oneself in the group, observe the norms, values, and customs, and interview members to gain insight of what the group means to them, and how group membership shapes one's identity and sense of self (Creswell, 1998).

Case Studies are also effective when one is interested in studying specific events. One can participate in the event, study human behavior, and observe the various themes that may emerge. Case Studies, as the name implies, deal with specific cases (Creswell, 1998). This is clearly not the situation in our study on religiosity, as we are studying religiosity with two different populations. Thus, employing this research method is not feasible, as it does not address issues on our research question and hypothesis. Furthermore, Case Studies can be time consuming and occasionally expensive.

Survey Research

Survey Research is most effective when you want to reach a large number of people over the shortest period of time. It is also cost effective, as surveys can be short and simple. Survey Research can fall under the Qualitative and Quantitative traditions, as the following discussion illustrates (Babbie, 1990; Schutt, 2006).

Open-Ended Questions

Open-Ended Questions are questions that allow the participant to answer questions in their own words. Participants are free to express themselves, and researchers look for cues in their body language and the

---

[7] Instead of being an objective observer, one embraces and adopts the values of the culture being studied.

words they use.[8] Open-Ended Questions can also be used in surveys, but researchers do not have the ability to read any nonverbal cues from the respondent (Babbie, 1990; Creswell, 1998; Schutt, 2006). Here are some examples of Open-Ended Questions:

1. What is your opinion on the illegal immigration problem in America?
2. Do you think that progressives are running this country?
3. Is race still an issue in the United States?

Open-Ended Questions are usually used in qualitative research, where researchers are interested in looking for developing themes. The main drawback of Open-Ended Questions through interviews is that they can be time consuming, and the researcher is limited to a small sample size (Babbie, 1990; Creswell, 1998; Schutt, 2006).

Closed-Ended Questions

Closed-Ended Questions do not allow the respondents to express themselves openly, but instead give them a list of answers to choose from. In most cases, Closed-Ended Questions are used when researchers are looking for frequencies and percentages of answers from a huge sample size. Closed-Ended Questions are best administered through surveys, where respondents can respond and return the questionnaire to the researcher at their convenience. Needless to say, there is a propensity for respondents to not send the surveys back (Babbie 1998; Schutt, 2006). Here are three examples of Closed-Ended Questions:

1. Do you agree with the government's handling of the oil spill in the Gulf Coast? (Yes or No)

---

[8] Most researchers employing this method use a tape recorder or video camera to record the interview. However, caution must be taken to protect the privacy and confidentiality of the interviewee.

2. Compared to other countries, the United States has very lenient immigration laws. (Agree or Disagree)
3. How often do you exercise a week?
   i. None;
   ii. Once a week;
   iii. Two times a week;
   iv. Three times a week;
   v. More than three times a week.

Looking at the scenario given regarding our study on religiosity, Survey Research appears the most viable, as we have limited time and financial budgets. We could also get a huge sample size by administering the survey in two different campuses. A religiosity scale can be created to test the religiosity of the two different populations, and we can look at frequencies and percentages of answers given through quantitative methods. Here are some questions that can be used in the survey:

1. How often do you pray everyday?
   i. Never;
   ii. Once;
   iii. Twice;
   iv. Three times;
   v. More than three.

   Religiosity Score: _____

2. How often do you go to church a week?
   i. Never;
   ii. Once;
   iii. Twice;
   iv. Three times;
   v. More than three.

   Religiosity Score: _____

3. How often do you read the Bible a day?
   i. Never;
   ii. Once;
   iii. Twice;
   iv. Three times;

v. More than three.

Religiosity Score: _____

We assign a religiosity score for each question and add them at the end. It is assumed that the more you pray, the more religious you are, and so on. We can see if the average religiosity scores of a private religious institution are higher or lower compared to a secular, public institution. Obviously, the higher the religiosity score, the more religious one is.

Comparing all the research methods explored, along with the research question and hypothesis and time and budget constraints, the Survey Research Method is the most viable method. Since we have established the research method used, it is now time to select our participants through a process called Sampling.

Sampling for Survey Research

Population is the group of people we want to study (Babbie, 1990; Schutt, 2006). In our case, we want to study religiosity among two different populations: one from a private religious institution and another from a secular, public institution. To survey the entire population would be impractical, time consuming, and expensive (Babbie, 1990; Schutt, 2006). Hence, we must get a Sample of the population, a segment of the population being studied. It is important to note that the Sample must be a reflection of the Population studied, as discussion on the types of Sampling illustrates.

Simple Random Sampling

As the name implies, this is a process where the researcher randomly selects participants to interview or fill out the survey (Babbie, 1990; Schutt, 2006). He or she may stand at the entrance of a library or a crowded walkway and select people randomly who are just passing by. This process may seem simple, but there is a propensity for researcher bias here.

Some researchers may feel uncomfortable approaching certain segments of the population and/or at the same time, prefer to approach other segments of the population (Babbie, 1990). For example, some researchers prefer to approach well-dressed individuals and avoid "hippie-looking" types, while another may prefer females over males. Researcher bias of this sort will inadvertently result in the fact that the sample derived will not reflect the population being studied.

Even if researcher bias were absent, sampling error can still occur (Babbie, 1990). Different segments of the population may frequent the place at different times from when you are conducting your survey. For example, a certain segment of the student population may use the library or walkways at different times of the day. Graduate students may prefer to use the library during the evenings, while student athletes may use the facility during the night after practice. Hence, you may not get a sample that reflects the student population through this method.

Another form of Simple Random Sampling is where the researcher randomly selects people from a Sample Frame.[9] Once again, this can be problematic—as in the case of the telephone book, you are only selecting people who have access to telephones. Similarly, selecting names from a student list can be problematic. Most lists are done in alphabetical order, and one does not know the class rank or major of the student, information that may play a role in the study. Though Simple Random Sampling is convenient, there are inherent weaknesses (Babbie, 1990).

Systematic Sampling

Simple Random Sampling is rarely used, and Systematic Sampling is sometimes employed. This is where the research selects, for example, every fifth person on the list to be interviewed—the sampling interval, in this case, is five. The problem of *periodicity*, however, can occur. Some lists may be done in a cyclical pattern, and if the pattern coincides with the

---

[9] This can be in the form of a list of names of students in the school or names from a telephone book, etc.

sample interval, problems can result (Babbie, 1990). For example, some may list the fifth person as a senior, and if this coincides with your sampling interval, your sample will consist only of seniors.

Stratified Sampling

Instead of selecting from the total population, Stratified Sampling ensures that the proper proportion is drawn from the population (Babbie 1990; Schutt, 2006). For example, if 20% of the student population of the university being studied consist of seniors, 20% of your sample should also consist of seniors. Likewise, if 60% of the population are women, then 60% of your sample should consist of women.

In the case of Survey Research Methods, the ideal sample size should be at least 100 from each population, making sure that the sample reflects the demography of the population being studied (Babbie, 1990; Schutt, 2006). In this way, one can generalize the findings to the entire population. Hence, in the case of our study on religiosity, we should get a sample size of 100 from each institution, making a total of 200.

Sampling for Non-Survey Research Methods

Experimental Designs

Participants for Experimental Designs are usually respondents to an advertisement looking for volunteers. Quotas can be used with regard to the types of subjects who respond, in terms of race, gender, and age through Stratified Sampling. If the number of respondents exceeds the required number needed for the experiment, standard sampling techniques can be used (Babbie, 1990).

Ethics in Social Research

It is important to conduct social research in an ethical manner, as the integrity and validity of your research can always come into question. Information gathered should be accurate and not fabricated or misrepresented. Most importantly, however, is the treatment of research participants. Institutions and organizations funding and approving research have their respective Internal Review Boards or Human Subjects Committees, which study the nature of the research and the ethical implications that go along with it. Proposed researches are either rejected or modified to meet with the ethical demands of the board or committee in question. When conducting a research involving human subjects, the following should be considered:

Inform Participants of Research Objectives

Participants should be told the entire scope of the research, its goals, objectives, etc. Deception should not be used to elicit participation, and the objectives of the research should be communicated clearly and effectively. It is the researcher's obligation to ensure that participants know what they are getting involved in, and that they do have the right not to participate at any stage of the research (Spradley, 1980; Schutt, 2006).

Do No Harm

Always consider the participant first (Spradley, 1980). Any research should not put participants in a dangerous position where physical or emotional harm is possible. Thus, participants should not be in positions where physical harm may befall them, or they are embarrassed to the point where it might affect their home life, jobs, etc. No coercion should be used to elicit their participation in any way, shape, or form (Babbie, 1990; Spradley, 1980; Schutt, 2006).

Protect the Privacy of Participants: Anonymity and Confidentiality

This is where you do your utmost best to protect the identity of the participants. There are two basic ways to protect identity: anonymity and confidentiality.

Anonymity occurs when the researcher is unable to identify a given response with the respondent. This can be achieved by telling your respondents in an administered survey not to provide a name or any form of identifier (Babbie, 1990).

This is best used in sensitive cases like drug use, sexually transmitted diseases, etc. as the likelihood of getting open and honest answers are higher. Anonymity also protects you from the possibility of being subpoenaed for the names of drug users by authorities, as you honestly do not know who the respondents are. Hence, you do not run the risk of a jail term for contempt of court or withholding evidence—more importantly, you protect the identity of the participants in the process. There is, however, one drawback here: you are unable to follow up on incomplete or contradictory information provided by a respondent (Babbie, 1990).

Confidentiality is where the researcher is able to identify a given response to a respondent, but promises that he or she will not do so. As soon as time permits, names and addresses should be removed from questionnaires and be replaced with codes or pseudonyms. A separate file should be kept in a locked box, demarcating the assignment of codes to each respondent. In this way, it allows the researcher to follow up if there are any contradictory or incomplete questions. The box should not be made available except for legitimate purposes. Ideally, once the research is completed, contents of the box should be destroyed (Babbie, 1990).

Nonexploitation

Participants should not be exploited in any way. If promised remuneration or reimbursement for their time, meals, or travel expenses, participants should be duly compensated. Researchers should consider what constitutes "fair return" where there are reciprocal gains. Participants should know that they can gain something from their participation and the data gathered from the research (Spradley, 1980).

Information Availability

It is important to make the information gathered from interviews, etc. available for participants. Allow them to review the information and make any changes that they deem appropriate (Spradley, 1980). In that way, they will know that the information gathered is not misrepresented. Involvement in this process makes participants feel they are part of the project and gives them a sense of belonging.

Conclusion

This chapter provided a cursory description of the various stages of conducting research and the various methods used in the data-gathering process. As sociology is a science, it requires a scientific methodology in the study of social facts.

Results of each study should take into consideration two important factors: reliability and validity. Reliability simply asks the question of whether the research conducted can be replicated (Babbie, 1998; Schutt, 2006). If so, then it is valid. If not, the findings of the research can come into question. Critics may attribute the lack of reliability to shoddy data gathering or faulty research methods. Validity asks the simple question of whether you are measuring what you are supposed to measure (Babbie, 1998; Schutt, 2006). It would be ridiculous for one who is interested in speed to measure the achievements of athletes on a bench press exercise, an exercise that denotes strength. If the research does not measure what it is supposed to measure, the results are invalid.

It is important to understand that research alone cannot answer every question pertaining to the social phenomenon studied. It may address one or two aspects, and open up questions on others. Results of the research may reinforce, contradict, or remain neutral on the research hypothesis. By no means is an inconclusive result an indication of inferior research. It may broaden the inquiry, asking questions that were never considered before. Hence, research may answer some questions, while at the same time opening up more questions for future social inquiry.

Sociological Theories
The Basics

Introduction

In studying any social phenomenon, it is important to adopt a theoretical perspective. Simply put, a theory is a proposition that explains a phenomenon in question. Theories provide explanations of how and why things happen, and tell us what to look for. In essence, theories are "covering laws" that play a role in our social inquiry through empirical research (Alexander, 1987).

In the study of society, it is easy to get lost in the wilderness of knowledge without a map and compass to guide us. There are many ways to read a situation, and it is easy to get sidetracked with inessential and extraneous information and avoid getting into the heart of the subject matter. Theories, in essence, provide us with a perspective—an angle in which to view a social phenomenon.

It is important to note that theories do not answer every question, as each has their respective strengths and weaknesses. We are enlightened by the insights each theory provides us, but at the same time we are blindsided by their inherent weaknesses. Some theories are better than others in explaining some social situations, and fall short on others (Alexander, 1987). Nevertheless, theories provide us with a starting point and a platform on which to develop.

Discussion in this chapter will cover the basics of three main theoretical perspectives: Structural Functionalism, Conflict, and Symbolic Interaction. Structural Functionalism and Conflict theories cover the macro aspects of society, while Symbolic Interaction deals with the micro. All perspectives provide valuable insights, providing different perspectives on the same phenomenon. Greater details are covered in the discussions on Karl Marx, Max Weber, Emile Durkheim, and Georg Simmel.[1]

Structural Functionalism

Structural Functionalism, as the name implies, explains how society works—how the different cogs in the machinery work together to form a cohesive whole. Jonathan Turner (1998) credits Auguste Comte (1798–1857) for the creation of Functionalism by

---

[1] Georg Simmel did not coin the phrase Symbolic Interaction, nor did he talk about it. Nevertheless, he laid the cornerstone for American sociology. Robert Park, one of the founding members of the Chicago School, was captivated by one of Simmel's many lectures. Symbolic Interaction came from American sociology, particularly that of the Chicago School..

comparing societies with biological organisms. Comte wanted to separate sociology from social philosophy by insisting on the application of scientific methods in the study of social facts, an aspect emphasized by Emile Durkheim (1858–1917). In the application of Comte's "organicism," works that followed (especially those of Herbert Spencer (1820–1903) and Durkheim) generally saw society as an organism that took on a life of its own. Discussions on the theories of Spencer and Durkheim in a later chapter illustrate this point further. The basic tenets of Structural Functionalism are as follows:

1. Society is made up of interconnected and interrelated parts, stressing the division of labor in society.
2. Parts of society work together to form an *equilibrium*.[2]
3. The belief in *meritocracy*, where people are rewarded according to their expertise and skill.
4. With meritocracy as the norm, *Stratification*[3] and *Inequality* are necessary.
5. Strong emphasis on *Order*[4] and *Integration*.[5]
6. Emphasis on *Functions* and *Dysfunctions*.

Here is a simple analogy of Structural Functionalism: Think of the university you attend. In order to get enrolled, you must apply to the Admissions Office, and upon acceptance, you go to the Advisory Center or respective department for academic advice. After that, you register for classes, pay tuition fees through the Accounting Office, and buy books at the college bookstore. Finally, you attend classes, and after meeting all course requirements, your final grade is given at the end of the semester.

As seen by the above-mentioned example, there are different offices that play different parts in the application process. Structural Functionalists argue that the different parts of the university are interconnected and interrelated through the division of labor. Each office engages in its respective area of specialty, and together they form a cohesive whole for the organization.

At the same time, people in the university are paid according to their expertise. The higher one's position on the bureaucratic ladder, the higher one is paid, and vice versa. Hence, there is stratification based on meritocracy in the system.

Any disruption to the normal function of the university is considered a *Dysfunction*.[6] Dysfunctions, according to Structural Functionalism, are viewed as sicknesses. In this case, members are mal-integrated due to improper socialization and require further education, retraining, and socialization. Hence, dysfunctional faculty, staff, or students are counseled, disciplined, or expelled in order to maintain smooth operation of the organization. Order is important here, otherwise *Anomie*[7] might occur. The best way to ensure integration is to have common values, goals, and interests.

How, then, does Structural Functionalism address social phenomena like social change? Some would argue that dysfunctions can become new functions, where new norms and values adopt and accept what was once unacceptable as the norm. The civil rights movement is an excellent example here. The protest marches and sit-ins eventually led to legislative changes through the Civil Rights Act (1964). Segregation and discrimination, once the norm, are no longer accepted and are now illegal.

---

[2] Think of equilibrium as a "balance" that maintains the status quo.

[3] This term was derived from the geological term *strata*, meaning different levels in rock formations. From a sociological perspective, stratification deals with the different levels (social classes) of society.

[4] This emphasizes Social Order.

[5] One who is integrated is one who fits into the system.

---

[6] Structural Functionalists view Dysfunction as a sickness, where members are not properly socialized to the norms of values in society. This can be corrected through proper socialization and reeducation.

[7] Normlessness: Without any social order.

Opponents of Structural Functionalism argue that the perspective is too macro and idealistic, suggesting that humans generally have the propensity to cooperate and work in harmony with each other. The theoretical perspective leaves very little room for individual freedom and choice, as it shows the dominance of society over the individual. It fails to adequately address individual motivations as to how and why they conform, and to what end. Though Structural Functionalism addresses why inequality and stratification occur, it does not adequately explain why people compete—and at times fight over—the limited resources of society.

Conflict Theory

Conflict Theory, as the name implies, stresses conflict. Theorists such as Karl Marx (1818–1883) and Gerhard Lenski (1924–present) fall into this category. The basic tenets of Conflict Theory are as follows:

1. Society is comprised of different groups with different interests, competing with one another for power and control over the limited resources of society.
2. Those who are in power manipulate social institutions to their own benefit.
3. The unequal distribution of resources.
4. Inequality is seen as a social evil, since it is a by-product of exploitation.
5. Those who are exploited are *Alienated*,[8] as they are no longer part of the process.
6. The problem can only be solved through the equal distribution of resources.

Returning to the scenario of the university as discussed in Structural Functionalism, the conflict perspective would argue that different departments compete with each other for funding and reinforce the stratification and exploitation of the institution. Universities are like businesses, and in any business, profit becomes the major premise. Profits are maximized by minimizing cost and maximizing output. This is best achieved by increasing the university's enrollment, but at the same time cutting costs by not hiring more faculty and staff to handle the increase.

On the administrative front, those occupying the higher rungs of the bureaucratic ladder are paid disproportionately higher. Those at the lower rungs of the ladder are exploited for their labor and expertise, and are not rewarded according to the output they produce.

For example, those working at the Registrar's Office and the Advisory Center get to deal with a disproportionately higher number of students compared to those working at the dean's or vice president's office. Though students provide revenue to the institution, it is those on the lower rungs of the bureaucratic ladder who deal with them the most. Some institutions manifest the exploitation further by requiring the lower-tier administrators to "volunteer" their services after hours and during weekends to register and advise incoming students, while their supervisors are exempt from such requirements.

On the academic front, some institutions hire teaching assistants, adjunct instructors, and lecturers, who carry the heavier teaching load, teach the larger classes, and are paid less than tenured and tenure-track professors—who teach half the load, are assigned smaller classes, and are allocated a budget for their annual conferences and research. Hence, from the Conflict perspective, universities reflect the exploitation of the workers through the unequal distribution of resources.

Discussion of the Conflict Theory brings Charles Dickens[9] to mind. In his famous novel *A Christmas*

---

[8] This term, used by Karl Marx, means estrangement from oneself and others.

[9] The novels of Charles Dickens were heavily Marxist in philosophy. Books such as *Oliver Twist*, *A Tale of Two Cities*, and *A Christmas Carol* (1843) expound the tenets of Conflict Theory.

Carol (1843), we see the dichotomous relationship of the "haves" and "have-nots" in the characters of Ebenezer Scrooge and Bob Cratchit, respectively. Though many see the story through the eyes of the romantic genre of generosity and the spirit of Christmas, the story is rich in symbolism when it comes to the Conflict Theory.

Charles Dickens.

The synopsis of the story is simple: Scrooge, a merchant, is the embodiment of the bourgeois capitalist, whose only premise in life is to accrue profits at the expense of his own humanity. His business partner, Jacob Marley, is already deceased, and Scrooge is left to run the company with his assistant, Bob Cratchit. Scrooge, a Social Darwinist,[10] is miserly and cares little for the welfare of Cratchit—or anyone else.

---

[10] This is best illustrated in Scrooge's famous words "Are there no prisons? Are there no workhouses?"

Work conditions are bad, as seen in the cold room and Cratchit's attempts to put another piece of coal in the fire. Christmas to Scrooge is just another workday, and Cratchit has to ask for the day off to celebrate Christmas with his family. Though poor, Cratchit makes the best of his miserable lot.

After visits by the Ghosts of Christmas Past, Present, and Future, Scrooge converts. He orders a boy to buy the biggest turkey in the store and to send it to Cratchit's home, and also promises the best doctors in England for Cratchit's youngest son, Tiny Tim, who suffers from a crippling disease. Most importantly, however, he gives Cratchit a raise, which improves his financial situation drastically. Ultimately, we see the end of exploitation through better income distribution and the better distribution of resources. Further discussion of the Conflict Theory is reserved for a later chapter covering the theoretical perspectives of Karl Marx.

The major weakness of the Conflict Theory is that it is too macro and takes on a materialistic conception in life. It argues that materialistic conditions shape a person's perception of reality. The theory fails to adequately address how individuals perceive and understand reality, and does not take into account individual choices and variations.

Symbolic Interaction

Unlike Structural Functionalism and Conflict Theories, Symbolic Interaction deals with the micro aspect of society, placing emphasis on how individuals interact, understand, and act in the world they live in. Developing from the seeds of German Idealism,[11] Symbolic Interaction rests on three premises:

1. People see the world through symbols.
2. People attach meanings to symbols.
3. People derive meanings through interaction.

---

[11] To put it in simple terms, German Idealism argues that it is the mind that shapes reality. The mind perceives and categorizes reality. Hence, reality is an interpretative process.

The caterpillar scene in Lewis Carroll's *Alice Through the Looking Glass* illustrates Cooley's Looking Glass Self model vividly. Alice has a hard time answering the caterpillar's question "Who Are You?" as her identity becomes unclear, with no reference point for her in an ever-changing world that makes little or no sense to her.

The key word in premise number three is *interaction*: stressing the importance of society. Individuals use society as a reference point for deriving and interpreting meanings. One's identity is also contingent on how society reacts, as Charles Horton Cooley's essay *The Looking Glass Self* illustrates.

Cooley argues that individuals see themselves through the reactions of others. They act according to how others react toward them and derive their image of themselves through others. Hence, society acts as a looking glass, reflecting the image of oneself.

By stressing the subjective realities of individuals, Symbolic Interaction argues that humans respond to subjective rather than objective culture. Hence,

Symbolic Interaction stresses that it is the mind that shapes reality, and that attitudes and beliefs can shape outcomes in the objective world. The discussion of the Thomas Theorem illustrates this point further.

The Thomas Theorem: The Self-Fulfilling Prophesy

The Thomas Theorem (otherwise known as the "self-fulfilling prophesy") simply states that "If we define our situations as real, they become real in their consequences" (Merton, 1968, p. 475). The premise of the Thomas Theorem is simple: People do not only respond to their objective features of the situation, but also according to their definition of the situation. The Thomas Theorem is simple. It begins with a false definition of the situation. Based on the false definition, people exact behaviors that reinforce the false definition, as a conversation between Adolph Hitler and Josef Goebbels illustrates.

Once the decision of the "Final Solution"[12] was finalized, propaganda minister Josef Goebbels had a vexing problem: promoting the right propaganda to win the support of the German populace. After all, the Jews had been an integral part of German society for centuries, and many were entrenched in local establishments and institutions. Hitler's advice to Goebbels was simple: Tell a lie loudly and often enough, and if there are enough people repeating it, eventually it becomes the truth. Needless to say, Hitler's instructions were heeded, and the rest was history (Payne, 1995).

In the discussion of the self-fulfilling prophesy, Robert Merton (1968) gave the example of the Last National Bank in 1932. The bank was doing well and its liquidity was good. However, when rumors of the bank's insolvency ran rampant among the steelworkers at a nearby plant, workers started withdrawing their money in droves. Though bank president Cartwright Millingfield (who had never heard of a self-fulfilling

---

[12] The Final Solution called for the annihilation of European Jews and other "undesirables."

prophesy) knew that the bank was strong, rumors of insolvency[13] would ultimately result in the bank's collapse. This eventually became true (Merton, 1968).

As seen from the examples given, Symbolic Interaction places emphasis on the human mind. Each individual, based on their personal experiences, would interpret the same situation differently.

Imagine yourself as a patron in a museum looking at a famous painting. Would 10 people in the same room see the same picture? Each individual is standing at a different distance and angle. Although everybody is looking at the same picture, each one is seeing a different image. Hence, everybody has a different perspective of the picture. Likewise, the same applies to society.

Different individuals have a different perspective on the same phenomenon, as their interpretive processes are guided by past experience and knowledge. Obviously, no two individuals have the same knowledge.

Symbolic Interaction, however, fails to answer the following questions adequately: If reality is based on an interpretative process, is there actually a reality? Or is there a "zero transformation of reality," and we merely transform reality based on our interpretative processes? These are questions contemporary social theorists such as Erving Goffman and Harold Garfinkel address.

Conclusion

Social theories merely try to explain a phenomenon in question; at times, a theory alone may seem inadequate. We find validity in each, as they provide us with valuable insights with our social analysis. Bear in mind that each theory is merely a perspective, and like all things, there are weaknesses within.

Some contemporary theorists have tried to address these weaknesses by formulating theories of their own. Each new idea provides new insights—yet at the same time, new insights provide new weaknesses, thus illustrating that social inquiry is in constant flux and is an ongoing process.

---

[13] This was due to the stock market crash.

The Environment and Population

Introduction

To understand the evolution of societies and the changing human-environmental relationship, it is important to understand the significance of the environment, ecology, and demographics of the population in their respective environments. Any director will tell you that the stage determines how the play is presented. Likewise, in the case of societies, the environment determines human behavior and shapes culture.

Ibn Khaldun observed that the environment had a profound effect on shaping biological characteristics and human behavior, and the same is echoed in Charles Darwin's theory of Natural Selection. Marvin Harris's Cultural Materialism looks at the human-environmental relationship, showing how primitive cultures serve a practical purpose in protecting the environment. Developing Harris's lead, this chapter explores the human-environmental relationships and the concern regarding population growth, overconsumption, and waste.

Botanic Gardens, Singapore.

The Ecosystem

In order to understand the effects of urbanization and population growth, it is important to study the ecology of the environment. As a discipline, ecology is the study of the interaction of organisms; between organisms; and within their respective environments.

All organisms live in the Earth's biosphere,[1] and within the biosphere, there are numerous ecosystems. A fish tank, a puddle, lake, and the whole biosphere are all ecosystems. Organisms within each ecosystem are bounded by mutual interdependence for survival (Thio, 2003).

As strange it might seem to some, all organisms in the ecosystem have a reciprocal relationship. Plants take in carbon dioxide and emit oxygen in the presence of sunlight. At the same time, plants produce complex carbohydrates through a process called photosynthesis. Humans and animals breathe in oxygen and emit carbon dioxide. Plants, humans, and animals maintain ecological equilibrium by keeping the oxygen and carbon dioxide supplies constant. Humans and animals consume plants for food. Inevitably, humans and animals die. Through the process of decomposition, human corpses and animal carcasses provide nutrients to the soil, which becomes a food source for plants.

As seen through the example, all living organisms live in mutual interdependence by playing an important part for each other: plants provide food for humans and animals, animals provide food for humans and other animals, and humans and animals provide fertilizers to plants through decomposition.

Since all living organisms live in mutual interdependence, altering one aspect of the environment would inadvertently alter other aspects as well. Marvin Harris (1974), in his study of the culture of reciprocity and humility among hunting and gathering societies, provides an illustration of this point.

One important characteristic of hunting and gathering societies is the fact that they do not hunt in excess. They merely hunt and gather enough for the day, and share their game with the entire tribe. With the culture of reciprocity as the norm, there is no prestige in giving and no shame in receiving. Successful hunters are also to remain humble, as rendering prestige would promote unnecessary competition among hunters (Harris, 1974).

As one can see, the culture of hunting and gathering societies helps maintain ecological equilibrium by not overhunting or overgathering. If the hunters alter one aspect of the environment by doing so, they stand the risk of killing off their food source. As primitive as their culture may be to the Western observer, hunting and gathering societies have a clear understanding of mutual interdependence.

When it comes to the environment, it is important to understand that natural resources are finite. Every ecosystem has a limited carrying capacity,[2] and overtaxing the ecosystem will result in population pressure—the pressure the population has on the ecosystem (Harris, 1974). In order to understand the effects of population pressure, it is important to pay attention to demographic[3] trends.

Workmen leaving Platt's Works. Oldham, England, 1900.

Prior to the Industrial Revolution, human population remained relative stable, with high fertility[4] and

---

[1] The thin layer of air, soil, and water on the Earth's surface.

[2] This is the ability of the environment to sustain itself and the organisms that live within it.

[3] Demography is the study of human population.

[4] The number of babies a woman will bear during her reproductive years.

mortality[5] rates. However, with technological advances in medicine, life expectancies have increased, resulting in a rising population. The fear of the Earth's population exceeding its food source was real during the 18th century, and this was best manifested by Thomas Malthus (1798).

Thomas Robert Malthus (1766–1834).

Malthusian Theory (1798)

Thomas Malthus (1766–1834), an English clergyman, published *An Essay on the Principles of Population.* Originally published in 1798, his essay argues that the human population will eventually outgrow its food source. Malthus's argument rests on the premise that food source grows mathematically, while human population grows geometrically. In the process, the human population will outgrow the environment's carrying capacity. As a result, wars, famine, and

diseases will result. In the process, human population growth will eventually stop (Malthus, 2008).

Upon cursory observation, this seems to make sense. After all, wars are fought over limited resources, famines due to food shortage occur, and diseases appear because humans consume less than the necessary caloric intake to adequately build a resistance to them. To reinforce this point, Malthus mentions two types of population checks: Positive and Preventive Checks.

Positive Checks

Famine and diseases fall under the category of Positive Checks (Malthus, 2008). This is where famine and diseases play a major role in population reduction. Discussion of the Black Plague (1348–1350) of the 14th century provides greater clarity to this fact.

The 14th century started off badly with a mini Ice Age. There were periods of unseasonably cool weather for the first two decades, which destroyed the crops, creating severe food shortages in the process. With demand exceeding supply, inflation resulted. Nobles and land owners still demanded their share of the crops, rents, and taxes, and farmers, unable to keep up with the demands, were displaced off their lands (Tuchman, 1978; Cipolla, 1993).

Many of the unemployed farmers went to the cities in search of work, which contributed to the already overcrowding urban problem. To make matters worse, preexisting sanitation problems were bad in medieval cities. There was no sewage system, and human waste was commonly discarded indiscriminately on the streets (Tuchman, 1978; Cipolla, 1993).

This was conducive to the spread of disease, and the problem was aggravated by the migration of unemployed peasants. With people consuming less than the minimum caloric intake, their immunity systems were low, making it easier for them to contract diseases. Prior to the Black Plague, Europe faced a housing shortage, inflation, and unemployment. It is easy to understand why historians described the 14th century in Europe as the "tumultuous century," as

---

[5] This is otherwise known as death rates.

anything that could have gone wrong, did (Tuchman, 1978; Cipolla, 1993).

The Black Plague, otherwise known as the Bubonic Plague, was carried by fleas that resided in the fur of rats. The effects of the plague were devastating, as almost half the European population perished. The catastrophe, however, brought about solutions to preexisting problems. And with half the population gone, unemployment was no longer a problem (Tuchman, 1978; Cipolla, 1993).

With population pressure relieved, food shortages became a thing of the past, and people were now able to own land and property that once were inaccessible to them. New solutions, however, brought about new problems. With the population halved, there were severe labor shortages, and there were insufficient people to tend to the crops. As necessity is the mother of all inventions, it forced people into innovation, ushering in the European Renaissance—the harbinger of the Industrial Revolution. As the product of the Age of Enlightenment, there is no doubt that Malthus had the Black Plague in mind when he came up with the concept of Positive Checks.

Preventive Checks

Delay in marriage and childbirth, along with abstinence, are measures that Malthus calls Preventive Checks (Malthus, 2008). Postponing marriage and childbirth has had a profound effect on developed countries. With emphasis placed on education and careers, populations of countries like Singapore are no longer replacing themselves. Holding immigration[6] and emigration[7] constant, the population is shrinking with each generation. Abstinence, during the time of Malthus, was a viable option. However, in today's society—though abstinence is still an ideal—the

---

[6] Immigration refers to people from without coming into a country to settle permanently.

[7] Emigration deals with people leaving their country of origin and settling to another country permanently.

practicality may come into question. In his analysis, Malthus failed to take into account the following variables: food-producing technology, medicine, and contraception (Thio, 2003).

Malthus predicted that human population will eventually outstrip its food source, as human population grows geometrically and food production grows mathematically. However, this did not occur. Instead, the food supply was able to keep up with the population growth. This was enabled through technological innovation, where food could be produced at a much faster rate.

Along with food-producing technology, improvements in medicine have eradicated and/or controlled communicable diseases, reduced infant mortality rates, and increased life expectancy. Hence, positive checks like diseases are no longer a means of population control. Last but not least, contraception has controlled fertility rates, and individuals are free to decide when and if they want to have a child.

Though the Malthusian Theory may seem archaic by today's standards, it does emphasize the importance of human-environmental relationships and the consequences of taxing the environment's carrying capacity. There are lessons one can learn from the Malthusian Theory, as overpopulation is still a problem that confronts social scientists and policy makers.

The Demographic Transition

The Demographic Transition is the theoretical perspective embraced by most demographers. It argues that human population evolves through various stages, a process facilitated by technological advances. This theory is modeled on the European population changes throughout history. The theory has four stages (Thio, 2003):

Stage One

This is the state of the European population prior to 1650. The population of Medieval Europe was relatively stable, with high birth and death rates. Life expectancy was relatively short, with the average life expectancy 40 years. Infant mortality was high, and it was the norm for families to have as many children as possible, as only half of them would make it to adulthood. Parents had little emotional attachment to their children, and many were treated as "young adults" and left to fend for themselves. It is not until they reach the age of seven that parents started investing emotionally and intellectually in their children. On the whole, the population at this stage remains relatively young (Cipolla, 1993; Thio, 2003).

Stage Two

This was Europe just before the Industrial Revolution in 1750. By this time, Europe was gradually moving away from the traditional feudal economy into capitalism, though feudalism still prevailed. Aided by the innovations brought about by the Renaissance, scientific advances in medicine, better hygiene, and sanitation increased life expectancy considerably. Birth rates still remained high, but death rates declined. Hence, there was a gradual increase in population. This is the demographic stage where most developing nations are now at.

Stage Three

Countries with high rates of industrialization are at this stage. Birth and death rates decline, and the population is older. The presence of a strong industrial base is evident, and there is a strong blue-collar workforce. Delay in marriage, childbirth, and the use of contraception are reasons behind the decline in birth rates, as emphasis is now on education and career. Nevertheless, birth rates still exceed death rates, though the population growth is much slower (Thio, 2003).

Stage Four

This is the stage where most postindustrial countries are. Birth rates are lower than death rates, and the fertility rate falls below 2.2, which is at the replacement level. The population is no longer replacing itself and is gradually getting older (Thio, 2003). At this stage, countries should liberalize immigration, especially to the younger generation, who are able to do the work that most poor people cannot do. The demand for young college graduates from abroad is apparent.

If the Demographic Transition theory is correct, modernization inadvertently would solve the growing population problem through preventive checks, mainly delays in marriage and childbirth. As countries modernize, population growth declines, relieving the population pressure in the process. However, new solutions also bring new problems. With modernization, consumption and waste increases. Not only do overconsumption and waste tax the environment's carrying capacity, they also contribute to a new problem: pollution.

Air Pollution.

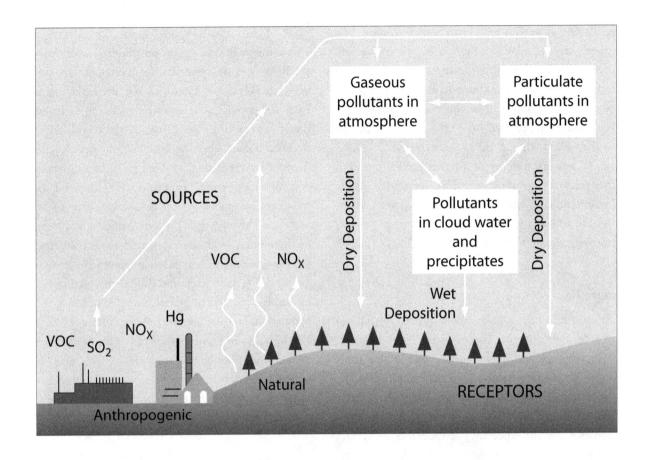

Origins of Acid Rain. **Courtesy of United States Environmental Protection Agency**

Pollution

Left in its natural state, nature has a way of transforming waste into other forms through a process of biodegradation. Biodegradation, however, takes time, and if we tax nature's ability to recycle by consuming too rapidly over a short period of time, pollution results. The effects of pollution can be devastating. Scientists have attributed the increase of cancer rates to pollution, citing increases in cases of bronchitis, emphysema, and lung cancer as examples. Some countries in eastern Europe have attributed approximately 10% of their deaths to pollution. Apart from health reasons, pollution could also lead to global warming, an issue hotly debated among experts.

Acid Rain

Cars are the largest polluters, contributing to approximately 80% of the world's pollution. Cars, along with factories, etc. emit sulfur and nitrogen compounds into the Earth's atmosphere. Chemical reactions in the atmosphere along with rain create a phenomenon called acid rain. Rain as acidic as vinegar has been reported, which can corrode limestone, marble, and metals. More importantly, acid rain can affect our food sources by damaging soil, crops, killing fish, and aquatic vegetables (Thio, 2003).

Global Warming Theory

Proponents of the global warming theory argue that the Earth's rising temperature is due to pollution, particularly the emissions of carbon dioxide, nitrous oxide, and methane, which all fall under the label of greenhouse gases. Greenhouse gases contribute to global warming through the Greenhouse Effect—the reason behind natural catastrophes such as rising ocean levels, hurricanes, and floods.

The Greenhouse Effect

The argument behind the greenhouse effect is simple: The burning of fossil fuels like coal, oil, and wood releases industrial gases such as carbon dioxide. Greenhouse gases,[8] unlike other gases, get trapped in the Earth's atmosphere. These gases, in the process, trap the sun's energy that would otherwise escape back into space (Thio, 2003).

The sun emits solar energy, and three things happen when the solar energy hits the Earth. Upon hitting the Earth's atmosphere, some solar energy is reflected back into space, while other energy is absorbed by the biosphere. Solar energy that is not absorbed by the biosphere is reflected out by the Earth's surface and escapes back into space through the Earth's atmosphere (Thio, 2003).

Greenhouse gases, as the name applies, play the same role as glass in a greenhouse. Greenhouse gases trap the solar energy that is meant to escape into space, causing the temperature of the planet to rise. With higher temperatures, polar ice caps melt, leading to rising sea levels and natural disasters such as floods and hurricanes (Thio, 2003).

Proponents of the Greenhouse Effect call for the conservation and use of alternative energy, less waste, antipollution laws, limiting populations—and most importantly—recycling. Opponents of the Greenhouse Effect argue that there is no conclusive proof that the Earth's temperature is rising, nor is

The effects of acid rain are obvious. This picture was taken in 2006 of the woods located in the Jizera Mountains in the Czech Republic. Rain, as acidic as vinegar has been recorded in eastern Europe.

there any evidence that the polar ice caps are melting. They also argue that the Earth's temperature is getting cooler, and that the use of alternative energy is just a deception and a manifestation of corporate greed. Needless to say, the debate continues. Despite the debates behind the Greenhouse Effect, there is conclusive proof of acid rain, a by-product of pollution.

As seen from the discussion in this chapter, human-environmental relationships are important. Primitive cultures have a symbiotic relationship with the environment, helping to maintain its recuperative powers and carrying capacity. However, with technological advances and the use of fossil fuels, overconsumption and waste have posed new problems and challenges for the future. The key question is what changed this symbiotic relationship to one of self-destruction on the part of humans. From civilizations working in harmony with the environment, human civilizations have evolved to one that destroys—rather than protects—the environment. How did human values change, and why? How and why did technology have

---

[8] Carbon dioxide, methane, and nitrous oxide are the three main Greenhouse gases.

such a profound effect on the human-environmental relationship? In order to answer these questions, it is important to understand the Social-Cultural Evolution of societies.

Demographic Trends

What do you understand from the following population data set?

Demographic Data	Japan	Singapore	United States	Argentina	Mexico	Zimbabwe
Life Expectancy at Birth	82	82	78	77	76	48
Fertility Rate	1.4	1.1	2.1	2.3	2.3	3.7
Infant Mortality Rate (per 1000 live births)	3	2	6	11	18	31
Crude Death Rate (per 1000 population)	10	5	8	7	5	15
Growth Rate (Percent)	-0.2	0.9	1	1	1.1	3

Questions:

1. Why are the fertility rates of Japan and Singapore lower compared to the other countries? What possible explanations are there?
2. Are the populations of Japan, Singapore, and the United States replacing themselves? What are some of the problems if a country's population is no longer replacing itself?
3. Can you make an educated guess as to which country has the oldest population?
4. Why is the fertility rate of Zimbabwe so high?
5. Can you group which countries are developed, developing, and underdeveloped?

Life Expectancy at Birth: The number of years a baby born today is expected to live in that country. Bear in mind that life expectancy is different from life span. We do not exactly know the life span of human beings, as we do not live under a controlled environment where we breathe the best air, live in ideal conditions, and eat the best food.

Fertility Rate: Number of babies a woman is expected to give birth to during her reproductive years. In order for a country's population to replace itself, most demographers agree that the fertility rate should be at least 2.2.

Infant Mortality Rate: Number of deaths per 1000 live births. Out of 1000 live births, (Infant Mortality Rate) babies will die.

Crude Death Rate: Number of deaths per 1000 population. During the year, out of 1000 people in the population, (Crude Death Rate) will die.

Growth Rates: Average: Annual percent change in population. This is otherwise known as Population Growth Rates.

Data derived from the International Data Base: www.census.gov

Social-Cultural Evolution of Societies

Hunting and Gathering and Horticultural Societies

The development of technology is essential, as maximum utilization of the environment is important to the survival of any society. Technology establishes economic life, and how societies relate to the environment. Likewise, technology also serves as a catalyst for social change, particularly the means of production, the political economy,[1] and the social structure the society has.

Subsequent chapters cover the social-cultural evolution of societies and how technology (along with the accumulation of surplus) changes human relationships. Five types of societies in the order of evolution are covered: hunting and gathering; horticultural; pastoral; agricultural; industrial; and postindustrial societies. In order to derive a better understanding of these chapters, it is important to remember the following:

1. The greater the utilization of the environment through technology, the greater the accumulation of surplus.
2. The more technologically advanced a society, the more differentiated it is.

---

[1] Political economy deals with the power structure of the society, and how goods and services are produced and distributed.

3. The greater the differentiation, the greater the specialization.
4. The greater the specialization, the greater the inequality.

Hence, it is logical to conclude that there is a correlation between surplus and inequality, where greater accumulation leads to greater inequality. As you will see, hunting and gathering societies are the most egalitarian of all societies, and inequality increases as technological innovation advances.

It is important to note that the types of societies mentioned are not all inclusive or mutually exclusive. Some societies, for example, do have characteristics of hunting and gathering societies, while at the same time practicing a certain degree of horticulture. Likewise, some pastoral societies do practice some forms of horticulture, and some agricultural societies engage in hunting, as well. Societies are categorized according to their primary means of food production.

Hunting and Gathering Societies

For the majority of human history, people survived by hunting wild animals and gathering plants. Change appeared approximately 10,000 years ago, when some started experimenting with agriculture. Over the

The Dayaks reside on the island of Kalimantan (Borneo), which is part of Indonesia. Some are also found in Sabah and Sarawak (West Malaysia). Traditionally a hunting and gathering society, their livelihood is now threatened by deforestation. To date, they still maintain their traditional customs and religious rituals.

last 10,000 years, however, hunting and gathering societies have declined significantly, and may soon be a thing of the past. Today, hunting and gathering societies are found in arid and semi-arid areas, particularly in Australia,[2] the Amazon jungle,[3] Southeast Asia,[4] and the desert regions of East Africa[5] (Lenski, 1984; Sanderson and Alderson, 2005).

[2] Australian aborigines still hunt and gather, and their understanding of the ecosystem is well recognized.

[3] Marvin Harris covers the Yanomami tribe of the Amazon jungle in the chapters entitled "Savage Male" and "Primitive War" in his book *Cows, Pigs, Wars, and Witches* (1974).

[4] Semang and Sakai of Malaysia, Kubu of Sumatra, the Andaman Islanders .

[5] The Pygmies, Bushmen, and !Kung.

Some anthropologists have placed fishing societies under the category of Hunting and Gathering Societies, as they technically engage in the same activities. The Dayak people of West Malaysia practice hunting and gathering from both the land and sea. Of course, carrying capacities in fishing environments are different, and certain degrees of social stratification do exist.

Due to the small carrying capacity of the environment, hunting and gathering societies are relatively small. They travel to hunt, and gather in small bands, groups consisting of approximately 25 to 50 men and women. Bands are connected through intermarriages, and together they form a tribe. Tribe members share a common language, religious beliefs, festivals, and cultural norms (Sanderson and Alderson, 2005).

The social structure is simple, with the family serving as the basic unit of subsistence. Division of labor is based on gender, and in most cases, the men hunt and the women gather. Inequalities and prestige are generally based on sex and age; veneration of the elderly is evident, as the elderly serve as a valuable source of knowledge (Lenski, 1984; Sanderson and Alderson, 2005).

Hunting and gathering societies are nomadic and travel extensively over a small area in search of food. Only 10 percent of hunting and gathering societies are capable of living sedentary lives. The necessity to move is apparent as depletion of food sources, along with livestock, will result if done otherwise (Lenski, 1984).

When it comes to the means of production, there is a lack of specialization since everyone is engaged in subsistence tasks, making technological advancements in other areas difficult. Specializations, if any, are based on gender lines. In most cases, the men hunt and the women gather. Since there is an absence of metalwork technology, tools are generally made of wood, stones, and bones and other materials extracted from nature. Individuals manufacture their own tools according to their specified tasks. Simple tools like spears, bows, and arrows are used to hunt and fish[6] (Lenski, 1984; Sanderson and Alderson, 2005).

For the most part, hunting and gathering societies live on a subsistence level for most of the year. As there is a lack of storage and facilities for the preservation of food, life is led on a day-to-day basis. Conditions are good when there is abundance, and bad when foods are scarce. For the most part, hunting and gathering societies are self-sufficient. Hunting and gathering societies hunt enough for the day, and rarely work for more than two hours a day. In fact, more time is spent preparing the food than hunting (Lenski, 1984; Sanderson and Alderson, 2005).

Hunting and gathering societies practice primitive communism, where resources are held for the collective and divided among those who need them. This is reinforced with the culture of reciprocity, where there is no prestige in giving and no shame in receiving. Harris (1974) reports that some hunting and gathering societies do not have equivalent words for the English "please" and "thank you" in their vocabulary, as it is one's social obligation to give and/or receive without conditions.

Goods are enjoyed by the entire group as a whole, although children do not fare as well as their elders when it comes to the food distribution. As there is an absence of private ownership and the accumulation of surplus, hunting and gathering societies are the most egalitarian of all societal types (though some forms of "functional inequality" do exist). As survival is critical, unproductive members are eliminated and selective infanticide is commonplace (Harris, 1974; Lenski, 1984; Sanderson and Alderson, 2005).

The culture of humility is another important facet of hunting and gathering societies, as undue praise and prestige to the most successful hunter would breed competition and overhunting, which would inadvertently kill off the food source. Both the culture of reciprocity and humility facilitate variance reduction[7] (Harris, 1974; Sanderson and Alderson 2005).

As there is an absence of any effective political organization, age and sex play a role in terms of social prestige. Respect is generally given to elders and those endowed with special skills such as hunting, warfare, generosity, and temperance. In most cases, prestige leans toward the venerable and those with extraordinary skills in hunting and warfare. Personality traits like generosity and temperance are also revered. Prestige, in most cases, is associated with political influence, and leaders hold their position as long as they meet the needs of the people (Lenski, 1984; Sanderson and Alderson, 2005).

---

[6] Some anthropologists would put fishing societies as a separate category, though they generally fall under the category of hunting and gathering societies.

[7] Hunters and gatherers depend on one another for survival, and their success or failure fluctuates. People give willingly, as they know that one day they might have to receive.

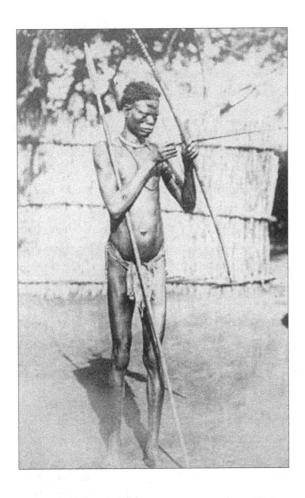

Mandu Man with Bow and Arrow. **The use of simple tools like bows and arrows are critical to the survival of hunting and gathering societies. The lack of specialization is also evident. They will share their game with other members of the tribe, and only hunt enough for the day. Approximately one percent of the world's population lives this way.**

Leadership is based on informal social structures. Leaders, otherwise known as "herdsmen," do not possess any real authority over others. Most of their duties are ceremonial, leading religious ceremonies and at times directing migration and subsistence activities (Sanderson and Alderson, 2005).

To date, only one percent of the world's populations are hunters and gatherers. With modernization and deforestation, hunting and gathering societies may one day be a thing of the past. Many are now relocated into unnatural environments, where their ways of life, passed down from one generation to another, no longer serve a practical purpose in the modern world.

Horticultural Societies

Horticultural societies are usually found in deep, densely forested areas with heavy rainfall, particularly in Central America, Southeast Asia, and the Pacific Islands. Although there is no recorded contact between the Aztecs, Maya, and Incas with the civilizations of the Pacific Islands and Southeast Asia, cultural and religious norms are remarkably similar. As the environment has a greater carrying capacity compared to the arid and semi-arid regions of hunting and gathering societies, horticultural societies[8] can sustain a larger population. In the discussion of horticultural societies, it is important to distinguish the differences between simple and advanced horticultural societies.

Simple Horticultural Societies

Simple horticultural societies are built on a gardening economy, with the use of simple digging sticks and hoes as tools. In many ways, they resemble hunting and gathering societies, but unlike hunting and gathering societies, they live in permanent settlements and are generally found in forested areas with heavy rainfall. As the carrying capacities of horticultural environments are greater than hunting and gathering societies, the community is larger with greater productivity per capita. With the greater accumulation of surplus, social inequality is greater with horticultural societies. Simple horticultural societies consist of more than one community, and intercommunity

---

[8] There are two types of horticultural societies: simple and intense. Simple horticultural societies are smaller and produce less compared to intense horticultural societies, where production is greater.

Akha Village, Northern Thailand (2006). **This is an example of a simple horticultural village, where people raise their own animals and gardens for food. Societies such as these are usually found in forested areas with heavy rainfall. As you can see, children run around barefoot and animals are free to roam as they please. The carrying capacities of such environments are much larger compared to hunting and gathering, and pastoral societies.**

ties are usually unstable and impermanent. On the whole, horticultural societies outnumber hunting and gathering societies by a ratio of 5:1 (Lenski, 1984).

As simple horticultural societies live in permanent settlements, construction of houses and other types of buildings are evident. Special buildings are erected for religious purposes, as religious ceremonies play an important part in simple horticultural societies. Horticultural societies generally practice animism and are extremely superstitious. As spirits live within nature, respect for the ecosystem is part of the religious psyche. Individuals with great oratory skills along with religious and magical powers are generally revered (Harris, 1974; Lenski, 1984).

Simple horticultural societies engage in slash-and-burn cultivation, where lands are cleared to raise crops and then burned when the nutrients from the ground are depleted. The ashes in turn serve as fertilizers and the land remains fallow for approximately one human generation. This practice allows the land to replenish itself, while the people cultivate in other areas. They generally use three plots, and move to another after 12 years. Hence, by the time they return to the original plot, approximately 24 years have passed. In most cases, slash-and-burn cultivation is devoted to a single crop (Harris, 1974; Sanderson and Alderson, 2005).

This is a recovering area of slash-and-burn cultivation located in the Kasempa District in Zambia. The ground is left fallow to recover, and it will take approximately one human generation before the land is cleared to grow crops again.

Warfare is another characteristic of simple horticultural societies, and is considered a way of life, with food production considered secondary. Due to the martial spirit, the rise of the warrior class was eminent; young men are trained for war from an early age. Male captives are tortured, killed, and eaten, while female captives become slaves or are forced to marry and work for captors. Marvin Harris (1974) argues that primitive wars, engaged by simple horticultural societies, are an effective method of population control, as warfare places greater utility on men over women.[9] As a result,

female infanticide through selective neglect occurs, reducing the reproductive capacity of the society in the process. Though controversial, the argument is viable.[10]

Higher levels of specialization are found in simple horticultural societies, with greater accumulation of goods. Tools, weapons, clothes, potteries, baskets, masks, accessories used in ceremonies, and musical instruments are made by specialists in their respective trades (Lenski, 1984, p. 123). There are also political, economic, and religious offices, which have greater staying power

[9] Though men are preferred to women due to the martial spirit, women in essence play a greater role than men in simple horticultural societies. Women tend to the crops, animals, and raise the children.

[10] Harris argues that cultures serve as ecological thermostats, helping to maintain the carrying capacity and recuperative powers of the environment. Read the chapters "Savage Male" and "Primitive Wars" in *Cows, Pigs, Wars, and Witches* (1974) for greater detail.

A Maya pyramid located in Chacchoben, a Maya site in Quintana Roo. The Maya were polytheistic and considered religious ceremonies an important aspect of their lives. Individuals bestowed with spiritual prowess were revered, and rulers tended to take on divine characteristics.

compared to hunting and gathering societies. Prestige is given to the man with the biggest garden and the most wives,[11] and the culture of potlatch ensures the redistribution of the limited resources in the society.

Potlatches are annual festivals where the Big Chief[12] gives gifts to the entire village. It is through giving that one acquires wealth, power, and prestige within the community. Prestige goes to the biggest giver, and the Big Chief remains in his position as long as nobody outgives him.[13] Harris (1974) notes that potlatches are primitive forms of capitalism and socialism promoting total competition, while at the same time redistributing resources from high-producing areas to low-producing ones.[14]

---

[11] Wives were considered a measure of a man's wealth.

[12] It is the Big Chief's obligation to look after the general welfare of his people.

[13] This is proof that social mobility is present in simple horticultural societies.

[14] There is a low demand for consumer goods in simple horticultural societies, as goods are generally shared through the distributive process of potlatch.

Advanced Horticultural Societies

The first advanced horticultural societies date back to approximately 6000 years ago. Most advanced horticultural societies are found in Sub-Saharan Africa and South and Central America. What sets advanced horticultural societies apart from simple ones is the use of terracing and irrigation. Some societies build canals and ditches in aid of their cultivation. The use of fertilizers is evident, along with metallurgy. Metals are used for knives, hoes, and axes, which increase the efficiency in the cultivation

Slaves were often used as human sacrifices in Aztec religious ceremonies.

of plants. Advanced horticultural societies enjoy a greater variety of cultivated plants and the productivity is greater, allowing members to devote time to other interests apart from food production. A Maya corn farmer, for example, could raise sufficient corn to feed his family for a year in 48 days. Surplus time enabled the development in other areas like building pyramids, buildings, palaces, and roadways (Lenski, 1984).

Advanced horticultural societies had a bigger carrying capacity. The Maya population stood at 3,000,000 during the ninth century, and the Inca had a population of 400,000 when the Spaniards arrived (Lenski, 1984, p. 146). With the larger population and economic surplus, advanced agricultural societies could afford to hold a standing army. Like their simple horticultural counterparts, advanced horticultural societies are very warlike. Wars are common, and victors subjugate the vanquished, forming kingdoms and empires in the process. With the co-optation of other groups, different traditions are brought together

to form a complex political machine with elaborate social hierarchies that mirror the feudal system of agricultural societies (Lenski, 1984; Sanderson and Alderson, 2005).

With occupational specialization[15] and the accumulation of surplus, trade and commerce developed. There is evidence among the Inca and Maya that a system of currencies did exist. Hampered by primitive forms of transportation,[16] trade was limited. Within the factors of production, advanced horticultural societies have a corvée system, which makes it mandatory to turn over a portion of one's crops to the rulers. Rulers, however, are careful not to overtax the masses, as many take pride in being benefactors for their people (Lenski, 1984).

Rulers take on divine status and at times preside over religious rituals and festivals. Advanced

---

[15] They had people specializing in making weapons, carving shields, tanning hides, and making potteries.

[16] Rulers had difficulty controlling areas in the peripheries due to poor transportation as well.

horticultural societies have a court system similar to their agrarian counterparts, with various levels of administrators. Unlike simple horticultural societies, however, their positions are consolidated and extend over a longer duration (Lenski, 1984; Sanderson and Alderson, 2005).

Conclusion

In the discussion of hunting and gathering and horticultural societies, it is important to note that the characteristics of hunting and gathering societies are not mutually exclusive and/or all inclusive. There are some hunting and gathering societies that possess the characteristics of horticultural societies, and vice versa.

Variables such as deforestation and development have forced existing hunting and gathering and horticultural societies to adjust, adapt, and in some cases, abandon the lifestyles that have been with them for generations. With innovation and technology, it is logical to conclude that the lifestyles of such pre-industrial societies will eventually become extinct. What is apparent, however, is the fact that egalitarianism wanes as surplus accumulates. This becomes much clearer in the discussion on pastoral and agricultural societies.

Pastoral (Pastoral-Nomadic) Societies

General Characteristics

Pastoral societies made their appearance approximately 8000 years ago, and are generally found in high, mountainous, desert regions where crops are difficult to cultivate. To date, pastoral societies are generally found on the Arabian Peninsula in East Africa, Mongolia,[1] Manchuria, and Tibet. Despite their geographical distances, pastoral societies show great cultural uniformity throughout (Sanderson and Alderson, 2005).

Pastoral societies herd animals over long distances for food. Animals like sheep, goats, camel, cattle, and horses are herded from one watering hole to the next and consume vegetation along the way. Pastoral societies move around in relatively small groups, between 100 to 200. Some tribes herd one type of animal, while

Mongolian children on horseback. **Picture by Vadas Robert (1972). The ability to ride horses is a matter of survival for pastoral societies. Legend has it that the Mongol leader Genghis Khan was able to ride a horse long before he could walk.**

others herd a few. The Mongolians also engage in hunting and see it as a form of refined leisure. They hunt antelope, boars, and wild donkeys and keep cows, sheep, goats, and horses in their herds (de Hartog, 1989).

The diet of pastoral societies consists of meat, blood, and milk. Pastoral societies are generally nomadic and shun land boundaries. Tribes move from one mountain

---

[1] Mongolian tribes consist of two groups: forest-hunters and pastoral-nomads. With the rising prominence of the pastoral-nomads during the 11th and 12th centuries, the forest-hunters adopted the ways of the pastoral-nomads.

pasture to another, and the distance traveled is contingent on the size of one's herd. There are times when pastoral societies have to abandon one lifestyle for another, when the need arises. Mongolian tribes, for example, have the ability to hunt in forested areas if required (de Hartog, 1999; Sanderson and Alderson, 2005).

Cows are used as beasts of burden and draft animals, and sheep for their meat, leather, and wool. Life is uncertain in most pastoral societies, and the ability to adapt to conditions is critical to the survival of the tribe (de Hartog). Tribes like those who live along the Nile practice subsistence cultivation, although on the whole, most pastoral societies shun agriculture (Sanderson and Alderson).

Agricultural products are usually obtained through trade with their agricultural neighbors. Commodities like flour, sugar, tea, fruits, and vegetables are obtained through trade. Other material goods like tents and clothing are purchased (Sanderson and Alderson, 2005).

Mobility is critical to pastoral societies, since the ability to move from one location to another in the shortest time period can be a matter of life and death.

This is compounded with the fact that pastoral societies are generally very warlike. Most pastoral peoples live in tents that can be assembled and taken down with great expedience. The bedouins and Mongolians still use tents that resemble those of their ancestors.

Stratification varies among pastoral societies. Some pastoral tribes[2] are egalitarian, stressing communalism,[3] while others are stratified according to the size of one's herd or martial prowess. Most pastoral societies are divided into numerous tribes with informal leadership. Those who are able to accumulate sufficient surplus acquire lands, and they become landlords.

---

[2] Mongolian society is divided into clans, which in turn are divided into sub-clans.

[3] Despite the hierarchy during the reign of Genghis Khan, the Mongolians would generously divide their food willingly with other members of the clan, especially during times of famine.

Mongolian jurts on the Mongolian Steppes (2004). **Picture by Yosemite. The Mongolians use a circular tent called a jurt, which can be assembled and disassembled at a moment's notice. The entrance faces south, as winds come from the north. In the middle of the jurt is a fireplace, which is used for cooking purposes. It is usually very smoky inside a jurt.**

Most pastoral societies are polygamous[4] and exogamous.[5] Members of the same clan or tribe are forbidden to intermarry, and must choose a mate outside one's clan. As warfare is a way of life, abduction of women is common. In the case of the Mongolians, there are no qualms if the first child is not biologically the husband's (de Hartog, 1999). On the whole, women play important roles in pastoral social life. Tribal chiefs seek the opinions of their wives, and it is not uncommon for wives to accompany their husbands during military campaigns (de Hartog, 1999; Sanderson and Alderson, 2005).

The Semitic[6] tradition derives its roots from pastoral societies. Moses, the person who laid the cornerstone for Semitism, was a shepherd for 40 years. All three Semitic religions are monotheistic—Judaism, Christianity, and Islam—and have the image of God as a shepherd taking care of his flock. Monotheism was logical, as it took only one shepherd to take care of a flock. The Mongols were also monotheistic, believing in the god Tengri, meaning "Eternal Heaven" (de Hartog, 1999).

Wealth and luxuries are shunned, as excess would hamper mobility. This is reinforced in the Semitic religions. In the New Testament, Jesus taught that one should share one's wealth, as it is harder for a rich man to enter the gates of heaven than a camel to go through the eye of a needle. It was also stressed that one should store one's treasures in heaven and not on earth, as one cannot take material possessions to the next world. The same is also stressed in Islam.

Genghis Khan (1162–1227). **Leadership in a pastoral society usually goes to those most able to lead in battle. Genghis Khan was able to unite the different Mongol tribes into a formidable force, which conquered most of the civilized world during the 12th and 13th centuries.**

"Zakat," as one of the Five Pillars of Islam, entails giving to charity, calling for the distribution of wealth among the tribe.

Ibn Khaldun, in his work *The Muqadimmah* (1989), argues that luxury corrupts. He admired the bedouins[7] over the Berbers. Khaldun based his argument on the premise that the bedouins lacked luxu-

---

[4] A person married to more than one at a given time. Most pastoral societies practice polygyny: one man married to many women at a given time.

[5] Marrying people outside of one's own group.

[6] The word Semitic is derived from the name Shem, on of Noah's three sons. It is said that the descendents of Shem resided in the Arabian Peninsula after the flood. Semitism deals with three religions: Judaism, Christianity, and Islam. Study of the Torah, the Bible, and the Koran reveal common denominators in all three religions.

[7] Bedouins are nomads, who travel extensively on the Arabian Peninsula. To this day, they shun land boundaries and live on very limited means. One of the more famous

Bedouins in the Judean Peninsula (2010). **Photo by Deror Avi**
To date, the bedouins still maintain their traditional nomadic ways of life.

ries, and, in the process, led healthier lives. Exposed to the elements, the bedouins had greater fortitude, were disciplined, and led much simpler lives. This is a general characteristic of pastoral societies, as most of them live carefree lives with high degrees of resilience (de Hartog, 1999).

Khaldun uses the words "character" and "fortitude" to describe the resilience of the bedouins. Compared to the Berbers,[8] who were urban dwellers,

bedouins were better disciplined and self-reliant. To Khaldun, this was the staying power of the bedouins: their ability to lead healthier lives with limited means (Khaldun, 1989).

To date, pastoral societies still exist, though technology has changed some aspects of pastoral life. Bedouin women are known to drive in the Arabian Peninsula, though many still wander the desert, scorning land boundaries. Likewise, in areas such as Mongolia, the nomadic lifestyles of the Mongol still

---

soccer players with bedouin origins is Zanadene Zidane of France.

[8] Khaldun was a Berber, who spent his entire life living in urban settings. As in most medieval cities, sanitation

---

was poor and communicable diseases rampant. Thus, it is understandable why Khaldun preferred the lifestyles of the bedouins over the Berbers.

Mongolian children tending a flock on horseback. **Photo by Vadas Robert (1972)**
Mongolian children learn the rugged ways of life from a very young age. Taking care of one's herd is essential to survival. Mongolians treat water with respect, bestowing it with spiritual powers, and do not waste it to wash themselves. Hence, Mongolians generally have a dirty look. Obviously, the practical purpose behind the custom is evident: resources that are scarce are used sparingly. This is a tradition that existed long before Genghis Khan in the 13th century. Notice the high mountainous desert terrain.

stand the test of time. Customs and practices that have persisted for generations still remain among the populace, and it looks as though change is not likely as long as cultures and traditions serve their practical purposes.

Agricultural (Agrarian) Societies

The discussion of agricultural societies is important, as it lays the foundation for the changes that came about during the Renaissance and the Industrial Revolution. Though agricultural societies existed on other continents, emphasis is placed on Europe, as it is necessary to understand the economic, social, and political conditions that existed there prior to the Industrial Revolution. This will provide a greater understanding of the Age of Enlightenment and the metamorphosis that occurred thereafter.

General Characteristics

The use of the animal-drawn plow ushered in the agricultural revolution (Lenski, 1984). The first agrarian societies appeared approximately 5000 years ago in the regions of Egypt and Mesopotamia. Others appeared shortly thereafter in India and China, and gradually spread to other regions of the world. Agricultural societies rest on agriculture[1] as the primary means of food production (Lenski, 1984; Sanderson and Alderson, 2005). Generally, there are two types of agriculture:

rainfall[2] and irrigation.[3] Most of Europe depended on rainfall agriculture, while other countries such as Egypt, China, and India depended on irrigation agriculture (Sanderson and Alderson, 2005).

Agricultural societies live in permanent settlements, where lands are cleared and cultivated. With the introduction of fertilizers, farmers were able to cultivate on the same plot of land continuously (Sanderson and Alderson, 2005). Furthermore, the domestication of new kinds of animals as factors of production provided farmers with new sources of energy and food (Lenski, 1984).

The growth of permanent settlements resulted in the establishment of villages, towns, and cities. Villages could number up to 100 people, while towns had a larger carrying capacity. Agricultural cities were centers of religion and government, with limited trade and commerce. The carrying capacities of cities were limited,[4] and most had a population of not more than

---

[1] Agriculture is farming, where crops and animals are raised for food.

[2] Systems that fall under this category depend on the weather for their water supply.

[3] This is where irrigation systems are constructed for water supply. In other cases, farming is done along rivers and estuaries.

[4] It was said that it took approximately 70 farmers to feed a city dweller in one year.

Picture by Charles Kerry (1917). The use of the horse-drawn plow was what separated agricultural societies from others. Farmers could produce crops at a much quicker rate. With the introduction of fertilizers, farmers could now till the same plot of land continuously. This picture depicts a horse-plowing contest held in Sydney, Australia.

100,000. Cities flourished during the Greco-Roman era and fell into ruins during the Dark Ages[5]—only to experience a renaissance between the 10th and 14th centuries (Cipolla, 1993).

Warfare was a chronic condition among agricultural societies, which were often plagued with foreign and internal unrest. Technological advances in production and military technology were essential toward the survival of the kingdom, as food production[6] can only occur during times of peace. Unlike horticultural societies, weapons are made by specialists, resulting in the use of armor and improved weapons such as the crossbow. The construction of castles and other forms of fortification was commonplace among principalities, and this in turn consumed a huge

---

[5] Some would call this period the Early Middle Ages. It dates from the fall of the Western Roman Empire at 475A.D. until 1000A.D.

[6] Enemies would often raid, pillage and loot, and burn crops as they wentg along,: resulting in acute food shortages.

Battle of Barnet (April 14, 1471).

living did not necessarily improve for the masses, as surpluses were enjoyed by the elites. The stratification gap from one social class to another was enormous (Lenski, 1984; Cipolla, 1993; Sanderson and Alderson, 2005). Lenski (1984) divided the European feudal system into the following classes: Governing; Retainer; Merchant; Priestly; Peasant; Artisan; and the Expendables.

Governing Class

Emperors or kings were the political heads and the governing class consisted of nobles who owned land. This group consisted of approximately 1–2% of the population, but they controlled half or two thirds of the total wealth of the empire. The nobles wielded immense political power and could acquire land and labor at will (Lenski, 1984; Sanderson and Alderson, 2005). There was also little distinction between personal and state wealth, and rulers could spend as they wished (Cipolla, 1993).

Retainer Class

The Retainer Class consisted of government officials, professional soldiers, and servants. They made up 5% of the total population and were the conduit between the elites and the peasants. Their job was to transfer surplus expropriated from the peasants to the elite. They enjoyed a substantial share of the wealth in the process. Though retainers played an essential role in maintaining the redistributive system, for the most part they were expendable[7] (Lenski, 1984; Sanderson and Alderson, 2005).

portion of the state budget (Tuchman, 1978; Lenski, 1984; Cipolla, 1993).

Travel became more extensive with the invention of the wheel and the horse-drawn cart, which fostered greater communication with other principalities. Territories of agrarian states are generally larger compared to pastoral and horticultural societies and have a greater carrying capacity. Some agrarian states have a population of 100 million with a variety of ethnic groups. As a general characteristic, agricultural societies lean toward monarchical governments through the feudal system (Lenski, 1984).

The Feudal System: Social Stratification in Agricultural Societies

Driven by the feudal system, agricultural societies are the most stratified of all societies. They have very limited social mobility. Although there were advancements in food-production technology, standards of

[7] Easily replaced by someone else.

As war was a frequent occurrence during the Middle Ages, the enlistment of women as soldiers was common.

Merchant Class

Merchants[8] engaged in commercial activities and played a significant role in the agrarian urban economy. Their rise to prominence coincided with the rise of medieval cities from the 10th century onward (Cipolla, 1993). Merchants were important to the ruling class; they dealt with luxury goods from abroad. As transporting foreign goods was expensive during that period, luxury goods were considered status symbols for the nobility. Some accumulated great wealth in the

process, and some ended up wealthier than the ruling class. Most merchants, however, remained poor, especially those who served the lower class (Lenski, 1984; Sanderson and Alderson, 2005).

Merchants did not command high social prestige and were considered lower than the ruling class. Those who were eager to adopt the lifestyles of the ruling class married into the nobility. On the whole, merchants enjoyed a great deal of autonomy, as many crossed political borders and dealt with other rulers as well (Lenski, 1984; Sanderson and Alderson, 2005).

Priestly Class[9]

The Priestly Class wielded great power and commanded substantial wealth. The Church acquired property and wealth through donations and was tax exempt. Monasteries amassed huge fortunes, and monks often embezzled charity entrusted to them (Cipolla, 1993; Lenski, 1984; Sanderson and Alderson, 2005).

Popes, cardinals, bishops, and wealthy monasteries lived like nobles, and the income distribution of the Church reflected that of society. This was especially true during the Pre-Reformation period (Cipolla, 1993; Lenski, 1984; Sanderson and Alderson, 2005).

Lifestyles varied between the upper and lower clergy, as their origins differed. The lower clergy[10] lived like the common people, as they were recruited from the ranks. For the most part, they played the roles of psychiatrist, doctor, and teacher (Cipolla, 1993; Lenski, 1984). Parish priests also performed administrative roles for the lower classes, who were illiterate. As one can see, there is an association with the words *cleric* and *clerk* (Lenski, 1984).

---

[8] Merchants evolved from the peasant class, where some chose to engage in mercantile activities in order to make ends meet (Lenski, 1984).

[9] The Roman Catholic Church was the prevailing dogma during the Middle Ages.

[10] For the most part, the lower clergy were parish priests.

Cleric, Knight, and Peasant.

The upper clergy,[11] on the other hand, lived liked nobility, since most of them came from the ruling class. Clergy at this level served as diplomats, officials, educators, and at times played a role in the military. Most important, however, was the fact that those in the upper echelons of the Church were able to forge political alliances, and at times have rulers under their influence (Lenski, 1984; Cipolla, 1993).

Peasants

Though they were the major producers of food, peasants were considered socially inferior, and in extreme cases, not even human by the ruling class. Approximately half of their crops went to taxes, and they wielded no social or political power whatsoever. Subjected to forced labor through the corvée system, many were exposed to inhumane treatment and the whims and fancies of their masters (Cipolla, 1993).

Attractive peasant girls were sold into prostitution, and wives had to succumb to their lustful masters.

Female infanticide was common, as girls were considered economic liabilities. Peasants were forced to live on a subsistence level with bare necessities. Their diet was poor, and most peasants lived in unsanitary conditions (Lenski, 1984; Cipolla, 1993).

Artisans[12]

Artisans were craftsmen recruited from the ranks of dispossessed peasantry, which consisted of approximately 3–7% of the total population. The majority of artisans were economically worse off than the peasants, and some were too poor to even marry. Artisans traveled extensively for work, and many were employed by merchants (Lenski, 1984).

The Expendables

The Expendables were the poor and destitute, who made up approximately 5–10% of the total population. They were the beggars, thieves, and outlaws who congregated mainly in the cities where the rich resided. Many beggars tried to look as grotesque as possible, as it would provide incentives for the rich to give them alms to send them on their way. Prostitutes, otherwise known as "courtesans," serviced rich men, and some earned a moderate income. Infanticide was common among the Expendables, along with disease and food deprivation (Lenski, 1984; Cipolla, 1993).

Mechanics of the Feudal System

In Medieval Europe, class was determined by social heredity, and statuses were ascribed. Though there was occasional upward movement, descent was more common among the populace. Figure 8.1 is the Feudal System flowchart modeled on Lenski's (1984) class division.

---

[11] This consisted of the bishops, cardinals—, and most important—, the pope.

[12] Artisans produced goods for general use, such as pottery, etc. Some referred to artisans as "unskilled workers."

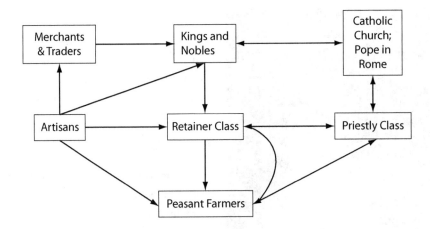

Figure 8.1 Flowchart of the Feudal System, according to Gerhard Lenski's (1984) class divisions.

i.   Kings and Nobles appropriated the greatest surplus. They ruled and hired the soldiers/knights to protect the Peasants.
ii. Knights protected the Peasants, and ensured political, social, and economical stability.
iii. Peasants produced food, and surplus was expropriated through rent, a percentage of their crops, taxes, and labor.
iv. Artisans serviced all facets of society and were deemed lower than Peasants.
v.   Merchants and Traders generally dealt with luxury goods, where Nobles were their greatest clients.
vi. Rulers derived their legitimacy through the Church.
vii. Rulers earned legitimacy derived through contributions.
viii. The Church received its income through contributions from all facets of society.
ix. Those of the Priestly Class serviced all aspects of society.

Life in Medieval Europe: High Middle Ages to the End of the Renaissance (1000–1750)[13]

Prior to the Industrial Revolution (1750), the European population remained relatively small and stable. Celibacy was the general practice, and delays in marriage were commonplace. Few medieval cities had a population exceeding 100,000 (Cipolla, 1993).

On the whole, the European economy was poor and income distribution disparate. The poor had no independent income and depended on charity from the rich in order to survive. Many of the poor were concentrated in the cities, where the upper classes resided (Cipolla, 1993). As mentioned by Lenski (1984), approximately 10% of the population was poor.

The threat of wars, famine, and disease was commonplace, and many lived a life of uncertainty during this period. The majority of the populace were concentrated in food production and there was little trade, save some weekly, monthly, and yearly fairs in some cities. It was not until the 10th century that Europe saw a rise in trade with the urban renaissance that occurred. For the most part, trade was concentrated in the cities

---

[13] For the sake of discussion, I am dating the Middle Ages to the beginning of the Industrial Revolution.

The contributions of women in medieval Europe were immense. Many engaged in nontraditional roles like running their husband's businesses and performing manual labor on the farms. The above painting shows women hunting, a role stereotypically reserved for men.

The urban renaissance of medieval Europe was due to technological advances that resulted from the growth of population (Cipolla, 1993). Though the urban population increased, it only consisted of a small percentage of the total population. For example, during the 14th century, London had a total population of approximately 30,000 to 40,000 (Cipolla, 1993, pp. 198).

Though the urban population was a numerical minority, they dominated the rural areas politically, culturally, economically, and religiously, as wealth and power were concentrated in the cities. Major occupations included, but were not limited to, officials, priests, scribes, scholars, merchants, servants, scholars, craftsmen, laborer, and beggars. There was also a small leisure class who derived their livelihood from rents, pensions, profits, or political office (Cipolla, 1993, p. 201).

Rent was high in the cities, and overcrowding was a constant issue. Due to poor sanitation[14] and hygiene, the spread of communicable diseases was common. In most cases, living at home was unbearable, and many sought to escape to the countryside when and if the opportunity presented itself (Cipolla, 1993).

The lower classes bore the heaviest burden when it came to taxes, and it was the peasants who suffered the most. On the whole, the masses ate poorly, falling far below the caloric intake necessary to build immunity. Most spent their lives undernourished and under threat of starvation. Plants were seldom used in their diet, and crop failures were common, as farmers did not have the knowledge to use pesticides and fertilizers (Cipolla, 1993).

The masses lived on a subsistence level and had very little opportunity to save. The rich, however, were able to save. Food, clothing, and housing were enjoyed as commodities by the wealthy. Monetary savings were hoarded, especially coins. Excavations in Italy during the 20th century uncovered pots of medieval coins buried under houses dating to the 14th century (Cipolla, 1993).

Monarchs made no distinction between private treasuries and the state, and they had free access to anything that fell under their jurisdiction. It is also interesting to note that the nobles, along with the clergy, enjoyed fiscal immunity. Taxes generally went toward the construction of military fortifications, communal buildings, and hospitals. The majority of the tax revenue went to military campaigns. Military campaigns were expensive, and sometimes consumed more than 60% of the state's treasury (Cipolla, 1993).

---

[14] There was no sewer system in medieval Europe. People merely discarded human waste on the streets.

In terms of the Factors of Production,[15] there was little specialization. Merchants played three roles: the head of manufacturing, moneylender, and trader. Wage laborers did not exist in pre-industrial Europe, and the employment of rational methods in production was nonexistent. Manufacturers produced goods from the raw materials to the end result, and they were not under any timeframe to complete the project. Women and children[16] also worked during this time (Cipolla, 1993).

Cipolla (1993) mentioned three broad categories of occupation in medieval Europe: primary, secondary, and tertiary. Primary occupations cover areas in agriculture, forestry, fishing, and mining, while secondary occupations encompass manufacturing. Tertiary occupations, on the other hand include banking, insurance, and transport.

Food production rested solely on the shoulders of the peasants, while artisans produced goods. Goods were produced from raw materials to the finished product by the same manufacturer, and commerce was limited due to a simple market economy. Peasants worked long hours to meet subsistence needs and to pay taxes to the nobility. Tending the fields was difficult. Peasants did not work for long periods due to climatic changes. Artisans, on the other hand, worked year round (Tuchman, 1978; Cipolla, 1993; Sanderson and Alderson, 2005).

True private ownership was achieved through seigneurial[17] ownership, where landlords established legal private ownership on lands under their protection. There are two forms of seigneurial ownership: patrimonial and prebendal. Patrimonial ownership deals with ownership that is passed down from one generation to the next. This ensures that wealth remains in the hands of the family. This is further reinforced with arranged marriages, keeping wealth at the same social class. Prebendal ownership, on the other hand, refers to lands owned by the central government and parceled out to peasants. Those from the Retainer Class were assigned to oversee production and collect rents, taxes, and surplus (Sanderson and Alderson, 2005).

Medieval Europe had a peripheral market system.[18] They had markets with marketing principles, but they did not serve as the primary basis of economic life. European marketplaces were called fairs, which were held on a weekly, monthly, or annual basis. The fairs consisted of merchants from all over Europe selling their products. Some fairs were held during religious festivals and feast days, which became profitable ventures for merchants and the clergy.[19] Markets in small cities were different. This was where merchants and artisans sold their products, though peasants did bring their harvest down to sell (Tuchman, 1978; Cipolla, 1993; Sanderson and Alderson, 2005).

Within the marketplaces, there was a lack of standardization when it came to prices. Due to the absence of a mass market, prices were determined through "haggling": the buyer asks for the price of an item, gets the price, and then tries to negotiate further. Unlike the capitalistic system where "time is money," haggling can be time consuming (Tuchman, 1978; Sanderson and Alderson, 2005).

Among manufacturers, trade guilds were formed to serve the interest of both the state and its members. It protected members from outside authorities, and officials had the right to settle disputes among members. Guilds also had the right to regulate the conduct of members, and forbade cooperation with members specializing in other trades. This inadvertently prevented the division of labor, which could have

---

[15] Factors of Production include labor, capital, natural resources, and organizations (Cipolla, 1993).

[16] Children made up the highest Dependency Ratio.

[17] The word *seigneur* means "lord" in French.

[18] This is a secondary market system, which is apart from the primary means of production.

[19] The sale of religious relics and bones of saints was common. Many would amass huge profits by passing off animal bones for the bones of saints. It was believed that the bones of saints brought protection and good luck.

enhanced productivity. Trade guilds also provided training for their members and regulated who could enter the trade (Cipolla, 1993).

The development of rational business techniques coincided with the urban renaissance of 1000 A.D. This was when the seeds of capitalism were sown with the development of the money market economy. Some principalities started using coins[20] as a medium of exchange, and basic principles of banking,[21] accounting, and insurance were implemented. Though money was a stimulus for trade, it was also a form of distribution and control (Cipolla, 1993)

Credit grew with the development of cities, in terms of deferred payments for goods sold, which stimulated consumption. Companies became "joint stock" companies, which facilitated the evolution of "stocks" and "shares" in the market. With the rise of the money market economy, cities gradually grew in prominence, which signaled the beginning of the end of feudalism and the rise of capitalism (Cipolla, 1993).

In terms of education, no one really knows the education level of the masses, though it is logical to conclude that most were illiterate. With high levels of poverty, undernourishment, and communicable diseases, many saw little utility in education. Literacy, for the most part, was reserved for the nobility and the religious orders (Tuchman, 1978; Cipolla, 1993). Literacy, however, increased as economic problems faced by the urban population escalated. Many relied on written records in a transaction, and this sowed the seeds of bureaucracy in the capitalistic system (Cipolla, 1993).

With the threat of famine and hunger lingering along with great fluctuations in prices, economic life

in Europe was uncertain. Furthermore, productivity was hampered with poverty, the lack of education, and the scarcity of equipment. Farm animals produced little meat, and performed poorly due to the absence of selective breeding. It was not until the Industrial Revolution that the economic disposition of Europe started to change (Tuchman, 1978; Cipolla, 1993).

The Demise of the Feudal System

There were combinations of contributing factors that led to the demise of the feudal system. Feudalism waned during the 12th and 13th centuries in medieval Europe with the rise of the merchant and trading classes (Tuchman, 1978).

Though not on a large scale, international trade was present, and the sale of luxury goods from overseas was a valuable commodity, especially in the cities. With the gradual development of the money market economy, the locus of attention shifted from the countryside to the cities. One can argue that the demise of feudalism was inevitable, with the Black Plague (1348–1350) providing the catalyst that ushered in a new period of European history (Tuchman, 1978).

Though the Black Plague lasted for only two years, the preconditions for the devastating plague were already set decades earlier. Everything that could have gone wrong in the 14th century did. The century started with several natural disasters, beginning with a mini Ice Age. There were unseasonably cold storms and rains, and the Baltic Sea froze over on two occasions (1303 and 1306–1307) (Tuchman, 1978).

The colder weather resulted in a shorter growing duration, which in turn created a food shortage. To compound the existing problem, the European population was already exceeding its carrying capacity, and existing farming techniques were archaic (Tuchman, 1978).

With supply unable to keep up with demand, inflation resulted. Food prices escalated, making it inaccessible to the general populace. The diets of many fell below the necessary caloric intake to build

---

[20] Due to the shortage of precious metals prior to the discovery of the Americas, coins were paper thin and were minted by being pressed against two metal discs. Minting was primitive them, and wear and tear of coins was common (Cipolla, 1993).

[21] The term "bank" and "banker" can be traced all the way back to the 12th century (Cipolla, 1993).

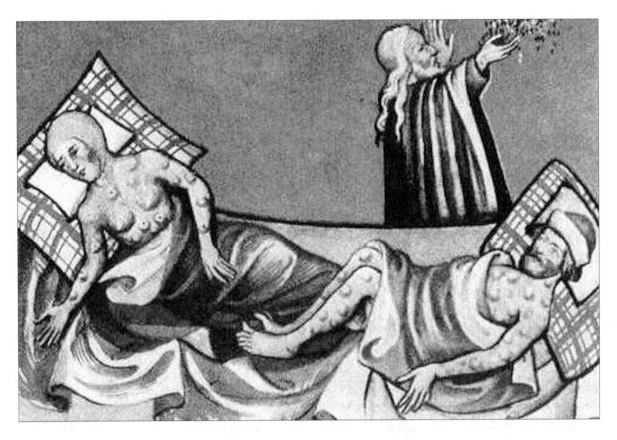

The Black Plague (1348–1350) killed approximately half of the European population. People developed rose-colored rings on their skins, and posies were used to cover the smell of rotting corpses in the street. There were too many bodies to bury, and monks resorted to burning the corpses instead. Hence, the nursery rhyme "Ring around the Rosie, a pocketful of Posies, ashes to ashes, they all fell down." Ironically, the plague solved many problems that had confronted European cities.

immunity, which made them susceptible to diseases (Tuchman, 1978).

Due to wars and the lavish lifestyles of the nobility and upper echelons of the Catholic Church, demands for rents and taxes from the peasants persisted. Unable to keep up with the demands, many were displaced from their lands and moved to the cities in search of work (Tuchman, 1978).

This aggravated the already existing urban overcrowding problem. Adding overcrowding with poor sanitation, the vulnerability to diseases was evident. For those who came to the cities in search for work, jobs were few and far between. Unemployment escalated and many were left wandering the streets begging for alms (Tuchman, 1978).

The Black Plague, caused by fleas that live on rats, ravaged Europe for a period of approximately two years, wiping out half the population in the process. No one knows exactly what started the plague, but the effects were clear. With half the population eliminated, overcrowding and homelessness was no longer a problem, relieving population pressure in the process.

The effects of the Black Plague also solved the homeless and unemployment problems. The unemployed filled in the labor vacuum left by those diseased, and the homeless were able to secure lands and property left by the dead. Starvation ended, as there were now sufficient crops to feed the population. Prices were kept low as supply met demand.

Though employment ended, the labor shortage persisted. With necessity as the mother of invention, people were forced to look for innovative ways to make up for the labor shortage in production. People departed from faith-based knowledge to scientific knowledge, ushering in another landmark in European history—the Renaissance.

On the sociopolitical front, the Catholic Church lost its legitimacy among the general population. Priests refused to administer last rites[22] to the dying for fear of contracting the plague themselves. The upper echelons of the Church left the cities for the countryside to avoid the plague, leaving the commoners to their own devices. Due to the shortage of priests, bishops of various dioceses allowed the administering of last rites by laypersons.

Suffering a huge hit financially during this period, the Catholic Church found creative ways to raise funds to support their lavish expenditures. Exploitation and chicanery[23] through the religious orders sowed the seeds of the Protestant Reformation, which germinated during the centuries that followed.

In summary, the 14th century was a catalyst to the following changes:

i. The Demise of the Feudal System;
ii. The Rise of Capitalism;
iii. The Decline of the Nobility and Aristocracy;
iv. The Rise of Merchants and Traders;
v. The Decline of the Catholic Church;
vi. The Protestant Reformation;
vii. The Renaissance;
viii. The Age of Enlightenment;
ix. The Industrial Revolution.

Discussion in the next chapter covers the advent of the modern age and the events that precipitated the Industrial Revolution and the changes it brought.

---

[22] Last rites is one of the seven sacraments in the Catholic faith. This was very important to the populace, and being deprived of such rites was considered worse than contracting the plague itself.

[23] The administering of *indulgences*, paying for one's sins, and the selling of religious relics (which were often fraudulent) were common practices among those in the religious orders.

The Advent of the Modern World

Industrial Societies

Introduction

Though catastrophic, the Black Plague (1348–1350) was a blessing in disguise. Problems like food shortages, overpopulation, inflation, and unemployment were solved with half the European population eradicated. New solutions, however, led to new problems. Though unemployment was eradicated, the human population could not keep up with the labor demands. This forced people to depart from traditionalism and seek innovative ways to compensate for the loss of labor, ushering in the European Renaissance (1350–1750).

The gradual departure from faith-based knowledge to scientific knowledge in human inquiry during the Renaissance was profound. Facts were no longer taken as absolute truths, and humans sought to understand the world around them through greater detail. The move toward innovation and science brought new inventions and the gradual mechanization of the forces of production. With the mechanization of production, another era emerged in European history: the Industrial Revolution (1750–1945),[1] a period that drastically altered the landscape of human history.

---

[1] The dates vary with historians., For the sake of discussion,; I will date the Industrial Revolution from 1750, starting

The Industrial Revolution (1750–1945)

If there was a period in history that showed how technology served as a catalyst for change in human relationships, the Industrial Revolution was definitely it. With mechanization and mass production along with the proliferation of goods, changes occurred in four main areas: religion, the political system, philosophical ideas, and culture.

Discussion in this chapter will argue that the Age of Enlightenment, Capitalism, Democracy, and Individualism were all facilitated by the changes in the market system brought about by technology. Closer examination will reveal that all four components mentioned complement each other, giving credence to how market forces can change culture. In order to gain a better understanding of the discussion, it is important to understand the social changes brought about by the Industrial Revolution.

The mechanization of production through the use of large machinery is a characteristic that distinguishes industrial societies from others. Commodities are produced at a faster rate, and the inevitable rise of

---

with the textile industry in England, to 1945, the end of World War II. It was after World War II that the United States entered the posti Industrial age.

living standards is evident. The use of large machinery saw the ascendance of factories, as machines required a centralized location to operate. With the rise of the factories, the demand for labor increased, as factories required people to operate the machines. The huge labor demand brought about a huge rural-to-urban migration, resulting in the growth of industrial cities. Unlike pre-industrial cities, industrial cities were centers of production and commerce. In most cases, industrial cities centered on specific products.[2]

With the mechanization of production, the use of fossil fuels as energy such as coal, oil, and steam was common, along with the development of metallurgy. The expansion of the railroad system and the development of communications brought goods and services to remote places, making commodities and luxury goods accessible that were once inaccessible.[3]

The commodification of the factors of production, and the proleterianization of the workforce by products of the mechanization of production, were features of industrial societies. Factories, raw materials, and land became the private property of the Bourgeoisie,[4] while the Proletariat[5] served as "hired hands" in the production arena. The use of rational techniques[6] ensured productivity, with workers controlled by the "tyranny of the clock." People reported and left work at specified times to ensure predictability. Through the division and specialization of labor, they had to work, to ensure efficiency. Subsequently, productivity is determined through calculability by the number of output produced and the time it took to produce it.

Social changes resulting from the Industrial Revolution were drastic. With the demise of the feudal system, social mobility improved, along with the increase in living standards. Social relationships weakened with the decline in traditionalism. Relationships revolved around secondary groups and interaction with strangers was the norm in industrial cities.

Traditional gender roles, which once played a practical purpose, waned. Work was no longer divided according to gender lines, and men were no longer the protectors and providers. More important, families no longer served as independent economic units, and became hired hands. The mechanization of production ushered women and children into the workplace, and both found new forms of independence by becoming wage earners. The fear of declining social solidarity and community was evident, and these are issues that are explored by major social theorists of the period. It was market forces that held society together, particularly through the forces of production in terms of the division of labor.

The changes brought about by the Industrial Revolution were drastic and rapid, affecting many aspects of society. People were not ready for change, and it was a time of uncertainty. After centuries of being in the agrarian system, Europe was venturing into new territories. People tried to make sense of the changes around them, and this was how sociology became a science. Social theorists like Karl Marx, Max Weber, Emile Durkheim, and Georg Simmel all addressed the effects and changes brought about by the Industrial Revolution. Discussion on each of their respective theories in greater detail will shed light on the matter.

There was not another period throughout history where changes came so fast and furiously. The Industrial Revolution altered the market system, which saw the

---

[2] For those who are interested, some nicknames of English soccer teams indicate the industry the city or town engaged in. Arsenal is known as "the Gunners,", as it produced and stored cannons for the Royal Artillery. Luton Town is called "the Hatters," as the major industry of the town was making straw hats.

[3] Buying foreign- made goods in your local store is a relatively new phenomenon. It was not untill the Industrial Revolution that foreign goods became accessible to the general population. The development of technology made the transportation of goods much cheaper.

[4] Term used by Karl Marx to describe those who have capital and own the means of production.

[5] Term used by Karl Marx to describe the workers. People who do not have capital do not own the means of production. All they could offer in the relationship is their labor.

[6] Finding the optimum means to any given end.

Child labor was common during the Industrial Revolution. Factories preferred children over adults as they were paid lower wages and were easier to control. Many were subject to physical abuse and forced to work long hours. Many children also lost their lives through factory accidents. If childhood is the age of innocence, that did not apply to the working class. It was such exploitation that propelled Karl Marx to write against the evils of capitalism.

demise of the feudal system and the rise of capitalism as the dominant money market economy. With the fall of feudalism, the aristocracy was the biggest loser, with merchants and traders the biggest winners.

The effects of the Industrial Revolution are clear. The causes, however, deserve some attention. The key question here is, what precipitated these changes and opened the floodgates to such drastic social changes?

19th-century housing for industrial workers. **Picture by Charles Rawding (2005). With the rapid rural-to-urban migration brought about by the Industrial Revolution, industrial cities were confronted with the problem of urban overcrowding. Many lived in squalid dwellings, and the less fortunate had to spend their nights on the streets.**

The main changes that came from the Industrial Revolution coincided with each other. The catalyst for change was technology. Mechanization of the means of production altered the market system, social philosophy, governmental systems, and religious and cultural ideals. As seen in Figure 9.1, the mechanization of the forces of production ushered in the Industrial Revolution, establishing Capitalism as the money market economy. Changes in the market system led to changes in social philosophy, religious ideals, governmental systems, and the rise of individualism as a cultural value. All the components complement one another, providing legitimacy in Capitalism, showing how market forces can alter culture and influence social relationships.

Capitalism

Aspects of capitalism existed during the Middle Ages, where people bought and sold at a profit. There was no fixed economic system on the macro level. Goods were produced from raw materials to the end product. Artisans produced goods on order and were paid a commission. Merchants and traders then sold these goods, where prices were determined through "haggling." Profit margins were generally small, and many lived on a subsistence level. There were, however, merchants and traders who profited immensely, but these generally dealt with exotic goods that were sold to the aristocracy. Dynamics of the marketplace altered, as the forces of production changed.

The mechanization of production during the Industrial Revolution, provided capitalism with the foundation needed. Goods were produced at a quicker

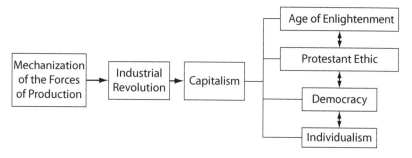

Figure 9.1. Changes brought by the Industrial Revolution

rate, and mass production facilitated profit-seeking motives through the need to sell at a profit. Adam Smith (1723–1790), in his book *Wealth of Nations* (originally published in 1784), discusses the effects of the mechanization of production.

Adam Smith in 1787.

According to Smith, the mechanization of production leads to the division of labor, which leads to specialization. Specialization in turn leads to productivity, as it allows workers to develop skills for their task and to discover better methods on performing their jobs. This saves time, which makes production quicker. Wealth, in the process, comes through the division of labor (Smith, 2000).

There is, however, one important proviso when it comes to specialization. It requires a large market, as a large market produces opportunities for specialization. With mass production and the call for consumerism, capitalism creates Perfect Competition.[7] According to Smith, the wealth of nations is not determined by the state treasury, nor is its spiritual and moral worthiness determined by the church, but by the total number of goods produced for its people to consume (Smith, 2000).

Two distinguishing characteristics stand out in capitalism: private ownership and Perfect Competition. Private ownership, in this case, is defined as the private ownership of the means of production. Factories, machines, raw materials, etc. are privately owned. When it comes to Perfect Competition, people are free to compete with one another, and one has the right to enter and leave the market at will (Smith, 2000).

Relative to the economy, Smith believes in nongovernmental interference. Capitalism should be laissez faire, where the market is free to take its

---

[7] This is an economics term, indicating free and total competition among those in the market.

own course.[8] Prices should be determined by market forces, forcing producers to make the highest-quality goods at the cheapest rate possible. As far as competition is concerned, capitalism promotes the survival of the fittest: companies that thrive should be allowed to flourish, while companies that fail should go under (Smith, 2000).

Smith identified himself as a moral philosopher and not an economist. As capitalism advocates total competition, there were concerns that capitalism would lead to total anarchy and moral degradation as the system makes competitors of one's brethren. Smith tried to appease these concerns through his work.

In the essay *The Theory of Moral Sentiments*, originally published in 1759, Smith argues that humans have the natural inclination to compete and look out for their self-interest, but they are also capable of making moral judgments by consulting what he calls an "impartial spectator"[9] (Smith, 2009). Smith does not pose a moral imperative, but instead argues in *Wealth of Nations* (2000) that the mechanics of capitalism itself serve the public good by contributing to the well-being of others.

Smith argues that capitalism provides its own moral justification by means of the "invisible hand." Since the market is propelled by competition, self-interested buyers and sellers seek the best deals possible. This, in turn, forces people to produce the highest-quality goods at the cheapest price possible. If producers make insufficient quantity to meet demand, prices rise. This would then induce others to come in and produce more.

If a seller charges an exorbitant price for a product, others will charge lower. Hence, free competition keeps people honest. In doing so, capitalism works for the public good, as it is in the best interest of producers, buyers, and sellers, to serve yours (Smith, 2000).

It is important to note that Smith did not anticipate capitalism to be as it is today. Smith saw capitalism as small companies and business owners competing with one another, and not the big corporations we have today. Neither did Smith live to see the time of large-scale industrialization, child labor, urban poverty, and hazardous work conditions. These were issues addressed by Karl Marx decades later.

Age of Enlightenment (1650–1800[10])

The Age of Enlightenment, otherwise known as the Age of Reason, was an intellectual movement that began in England during the 17th century, and developed in France during the 18th century. It departed from the faith-based (irrational) knowledge of the medieval age to scientific (rational) knowledge. It was the age that required individuals to depart from their inability to use reason without the guidance of others and have the courage to use one's own reason. Despite the different philosophical tenets that developed during this period, Empiricism, Rationalism, German Idealism, British Utilitarianism, and Positivism have the following common denominators:

1. Reason as man's central capacity.
2. Man is rational and by nature inherently good.
3. Individual and humanity can progress to perfection.
4. All individuals have equal capacity in respect to their rationality, and hence should be granted equality under the law.
5. Tolerance should be granted toward others and their ways of life.
6. Beliefs should only be accepted on the basis of reason.
7. Devalues local prejudices and customs.

---

[8] Adam Smith is well known for the phrase "Let the invisible hand guide the economy."

[9] This is similar to the superego in Sigmund Freud's theory of psychoanalysis.

[10] It is not clear when or if the Age of Enlightenment actually ended. I chose 1800, as it was the beginning of the Victorian age in England.

8. Plays down nonrational aspects of nature. Education should provide knowledge and not mold character.

(Honderich, 1995, p. 236)

Empiricism argues that knowledge is gained through experience acquired through sensory perception of the physical world, while Rationalism takes the position that the mind has knowledge beyond the sensory experience. Idealism, on the other hand, bases its premise on the fact that the mind shapes reality, while British Utilitarianism seeks utility in any social transaction (advocating the greatest happiness for the greatest number), while Positivism calls for the use of scientific knowledge and methods in social inquiry.

All these philosophical ideas departed from traditionalism and complemented the capitalistic economic model. For one, they called for the use of rational techniques,[11] acknowledged the power of the individual, and supported self-interest and self-gain. Discussion will cover the philosophical ideas mentioned in greater detail.

British Empiricism[12]

British Empiricism is based on one's perceptual encounter of the world, where one's knowledge is derived through experience acquired through sensory experiences. As the name implies, Empiricists place emphasis on the material world and the senses as the form of affirmation and verification of the truth. John Locke (1632–1704) argues that children are a *tabula rasa*[13] when they are born. Void of any information, children acquire knowledge through sensory experience (Honderich, 1995; Mannion, 2006).

The influences that John Locke had on America's founding fathers were significant. Locke argues that

John Locke in 1697.

humans had inalienable rights in the pursuit of life, liberty, and happiness. In terms of one's relationship with the government, Locke maintains that society has a "natural state" of violence and barbarianism. It is the government's obligation to prevent society's regression to its natural state (Honderich, 1995; Mannion, 2006).

In doing so, the government ensures the greater good of society. Most importantly, however, in maintaining the greater good, the government should not compromise the rights of the individual. If the people are unhappy with the government, they can leave the country, challenge it, or change it: a principle taken to heart by those who participated in the American (1776) and French (1789) revolutions (Honderich, 1995; Mannion, 2006).

British Empiricism was embraced by the European discourse due to its relationship to science and verification of truth through empirical evidence. Empiricism substantiates knowledge through observation, and the

---

[11] Looking for the optimum means to any given end.

[12] Empiricism is best summarized this way: what I can see, touch, feel, smell, and hear is real.

[13] "Blank slate" in Latin.

validity of observations is contingent on procedures employed (Honderich, 1995; Mannion, 2006). Furthermore, British Empiricism complemented the basic tenets of capitalism—it is a system of producing goods and services for the greater good, with individual profit as the primary motive.

Rationalism[14]

Rationalism argues that reality extends beyond the sensory experience, giving credence to the power of the human mind in shaping and understanding reality. René Descartes (1596–1650), known as the father of modern philosophy, calls for skepticism—that people should doubt everything they know according to the senses. There is a possibility that our senses may be deceptive, and to build one's knowledge solely out of one's senses is shortsighted. Needless to say, this ran counter to the British Empiricists (Honderich, 1995; Mannion, 2006).

After all, no one is sure if we are actually living a reality or if we are in a dream. This is Descartes's "Dream Hypothesis," wherein he argues that what we are living is a dream and that the physical world is merely an extension of the dream and not reality. There is also a possibility that we are being deceived by a malignant demon into believing what is real when it is not. This is Descartes's "Demon Hypothesis" (Honderich, 1995; Mannion, 2006).

Descartes's answer to existence is the famous quote "Cogito ergo sum," meaning "I think, therefore I am" in Latin. What is absolute to Descartes, is the existence of the thinker. Thus, self-awareness becomes the essence of one's existence (Honderich, 1995; Mannion, 2006).

Descartes posits that there are two elements called "substances" that compose reality. Thinking Substances are the mind, while Extended Substances constitute the body. All ideas do not originate from

René Descartes (1596–1650).

the senses, as other ideas, which are accessible, are stored in the mind. Ideas that are stored in the mind are termed "innate." Innate ideas (primary) constitute things like mathematics, physics, and morality (Honderich, 1995; Mannion, 2006).

There are two more ideas, apart from innate ideas: "adventitious" (secondary), which comes from experience, and "fictitious," what is not true. People start with what is called innate knowledge, and then proceed with secondary knowledge through experience. In summation, according to Descartes and other Rationalists, knowledge is acquired through reason (Honderich, 1995; Mannion, 2006).

German Idealism[15]

German Idealism argues that it is the mind that shapes reality. Unlike the Empiricists, who argue that knowledge is derived through sensory experiences,

---

[14] Rationalism argues that knowledge can be derived without sensory experiences.

[15] Idealism argues that it is the mind that shapes reality.

and the Rationalists, who believe that knowledge is acquired through reason, German Idealists such as Immanuel Kant (1724–1804) argue that perception is reality (Mannion, 2006).

According to Kant, the mind has categories of understanding as it has the ability to catalog, codify, and make sense of the world. In essence, it is the individual mind that makes sense and creates reality. Kant defines two types of judgments: analytic and synthetic (Honderich, 1995; Mannion, 2006).

Analytic truth is truth that can be determined within itself. Kant gives the example of analytic truth in the sentence: "All black horses are horses." As seen in the sentence, one can find the truth within the

Immanuel Kant (1724–1804). **German Idealists such as Immanuel Kant believed that perception is reality.**

sentence. After all, horses—whether black or not—are horses, and one does not have to look any further to find the answer. This is what Kant calls an "a priori" judgment, as one does not have to rely on the senses to draw the conclusion that all black horses are horses (Honderich, 1995; Mannion, 2006).

Synthetic judgments, on the other hand, are determined by relying on one's sense to make a determination. Kant's example here is the sentence: "Look, the horse is black." One has to look before making a judgment, and this judgment is what Kant terms as an "a posteriori" judgment (Honderich, 1995; Mannion, 2006).

Georg W. Hegel (1770–1831) was one of the most influential philosophers of his time, best known for his "dialectics." Hegel believes that the Absolute is the human mind and its ability to reason. As ideas are by-products of reason, ideas are never constant and are ever evolving. To Hegel, it is ideas that shape reality and material conditions. Change occurs when there is a contradiction (Honderich, 1995; Mannion, 2006).

Any idea presents a "thesis" (a proposition), and any idea will eventually meet an "antithesis" (an opposing proposition). When this occurs, we have a contradiction. When a contradiction occurs, a new idea evolves: "a synthesis." Hence, contradictions in opposing ideas will bring forth a new idea. The synthesis becomes a new thesis, and a new thesis will meet with a new antithesis, and so on. Thus, change comes through contradictions (Honderich, 1995; Mannion, 2006). The influence of Hegel's philosophy was profound and laid the cornerstone for Karl Marx, author of *The Communist Manifesto* (1848).

British Utilitarianism[16]

The best-known British Utilitarian is Jeremy Bentham (1748–1832). British Utilitarianism believes that

---

[16] Utilitarianism treats pleasure and the desire principle as the sole element of human good. Any consequence of any act should result in the greatest happiness for the greatest number.

mankind's gravitation is to the utility of any function. This is consistent with capitalism as it seeks maximum gains, but this time in pleasure. The premise of Utilitarianism is based on the premise that morality is measured according to the greatest happiness to the greatest number (Bentham 2000). John Stuart Mill (1808–1873) echoes the same sentiment, stating that it is every individual's right to pursue pleasure and happiness, but stresses personal responsibility (Honderich, 1995; Mannion, 2006).

What society considers as pleasure and comfort should be the norm, so long as no harm is done. As morality and happiness are related, the greater the happiness a deed provides, the more moral it is, and vice versa. According to Mill, governmental influence on the affairs of the individual should be minimal, unless the individual presents a clear and present danger to others. Everyone is entitled to free speech, but no harm should be the result of it (Honderich, 1995; Bentham; 2000; Mannion, 2006).

Unlike German Idealism (i.e., individualistic in nature), British Utilitarianism takes the collective whole into consideration, as laws and public policies should serve the greater good. Utilitarianism's doctrine has played a major role in democratic and political reforms (Honderich, 1995; Bentham; 2000; Mannion, 2006).

The influence of British Utilitarianism on American jurisprudence is significant. For one thing, British Utilitarianism maintains that all human beings are inherently good,[17] and that the protection of the innocent should take precedence over the punishment of the guilty—hence, the assumption that the accused is presumed innocent until proven guilty beyond a reasonable doubt. When a person is found guilty, the punishment should not be too severe, as it merely serves as a deterrent contingent on the nature of the

Jeremy Bentham (1748–1832). Three days after his death, according to his wishes, Jeremy Bentham's body was publicly dissected by his doctor, then mummified and placed in a glass box that sits in the boardroom of University College of London, England. He had one condition when he donated his fortune to the school: that he must attend every Board of Trustees meeting in perpetuity. He felt that his body would serve greater utility this way than buried.

offense. Hence, the punishment should always fit the crime[18] (Bentham, 2000; Mannion, 2006).

---

[17] This is based on the assumption that men are rational and inherently good.

[18] It is also interesting to note that the United States is one of the few countries in the world that has solitary confinement in its prison system. The major premise of solitary confinement comes from the principles of Utilitarianism, where individuals, if left alone, would spend time contemplating the consequences of their crime, and would change their

Positivism

This is the philosophy associated with Auguste Comte,[19] whose doctrine emerged during the latter half of the 19th century. Though Comte wrote his treatise on Positivism in 1830, the philosophy came into prominence two decades later when it launched a full-scale assault on German Idealism (Honderich, 1995; Morrison, 2006).

Comte argues that speculative and intuitive knowledge are archaic and should be replaced with Positivism, which, according to Comte, is the highest form of knowledge. In his "Law of Three Stages," Comte argues that human knowledge evolves from the "theological," "metaphysical," and finally to the "scientific stage." Knowledge derived from the theological stage is derived from "faith-based" knowledge, metaphysical on logic, and scientific through the use of scientific methods in observation and verification of facts (Honderich, 1995; Morrison, 2006).

Accepting the methods used by physical science as a model of certainty, Comte calls for the use of scientific methods in studying any social phenomenon. With observation as the criteria for verification, Comte calls for law-like regularities when it comes to the search for truth. In essence, Positivism calls for a scientific worldview, putting theory with observable empirical evidence as social facts (Morrison, 2006). One can argue that the seeds of sociology as a social science came from the French tradition of Positivism.

The philosophical perspectives of the Age of Enlightenment had profound effects in the development of the modern world. All of them questioned and tore away from traditional beliefs that had existed for centuries. These philosophies provided individuals with autonomy and promoted the culture of individualism. This was the value Alexis de Tocqueville saw as

necessary in the modern age, as the market and social systems had changed. He summarily predicted that America would be the next power, as it had the value system that drove the engine of capitalism to its fullest.

The Protestant Reformation (1350–1750)[20]

The effects of the Black Plague (1348–1350) were profound on the Catholic Church. With the decline of the feudal system, the Church lost its financial base, with the European aristocracy contributing less financially. With priests refusing to administer last rites to the dying during the plague, legitimacy waned. With the loss of finances, the Church engaged in "creative financing" to make up for losses in income and charged "indulgences" in the sacrament of penance. This led to Martin Luther's (1483–1546) outrage, which he demonstrated by posting his 95 Theses on a church door—the landmark in the Protestant Reformation. Martin Luther and John Calvin (1509–1564) laid the foundations for the Protestant Ethic, as further discussion illustrates.

Changes in the market forces also contributed to the Protestant Reformation. Different perceptions in social philosophy in capitalism propelled the departure from traditionalism. Archaic doctrines of the Catholic Church now became antiquated in the face of change; the Church could no longer keep up with the changing landscape of Europe. In essence, the Protestant Reformation was inevitable as society moved from faith-based to scientific knowledge.

The tenets of the Protestant faith turned the Catholic doctrine of Contemptus Mundi[21] on its head. Striving to undo the tenets of the Catholic faith,

---

ways in the process. Once again, it is based on the premise that people are inherently good.

[19] This movement was spearheaded by Henri de Saint-Simon. Comte was Saint-Simon's secretary in his younger days.

[20] The dates of the Protestant Reformation vary among historians, as it is difficult to pinpoint its exact start and end. For the sake of discussion, I dated the beginning of the Protestant Reformation at the end of the Black Plague (1348–1350), and the end as the beginning of the Industrial Revolution.

[21] Meaning "Contempt for the World" in Latin.

Martin Luther (1483–1546). **Martin Luther believed that the Bible should be interpreted literally and that one's worldly occupation is seen as God's "calling." Luther is best known for his 95 Theses against the Catholic Church.**

the Protestant doctrine contradicted the Catholic dogma with its own interpretations of the individual's relationship with God. It is interesting to note that the tenets of the Protestant faith complemented capitalism, providing individuals with the moral energy to do well in the market place.

According to the Catholic tradition, the world was seen as an evil place, as God gave the devil domain over the world after the fall of Adam and Eve from the Garden of Eden. Hence, anything of this world was considered evil. Wealth and luxury were seen as distraction from one's devotion to God, and anything that brought pleasures of the flesh was sinful. Catholics practiced "otherworldly asceticism,"[22] where hatred of this world would lead to glory in the next.

The Protestants, however, did not see the world as an evil place. God is good, so everything that is created by God must also be good. Thus, the world was seen as a sign of God's glory. One can enjoy heaven while on this Earth. Success is seen as a mark of God's blessing, and failure as God's curse. Unlike the Catholics who strove to see God in the next world, Protestants believed that one develops a personal relationship with God while on this Earth, emphasizing the inner experience of faith through prayer.

Martin Luther saw all worldly occupations as religious "callings." John Calvin (1509–1564) came up with the doctrine of Predestination (Doctrine of the Elect), where one's place in heaven or hell is already preordained by God. Therefore, one's obligation while on Earth is to win God's favor, and this is achieved through the Protestant Work Ethic. God's blessings are seen through one's economic success, while God's wrath brings ill fortune and failure. Success is seen, then, as a virtue. The following are some examples of the Protestant Ethic:

1. Hard Work;
2. Discipline;
3. Perseverance;
4. Patience;
5. Humility;
6. Frugality;
7. Honesty;
8. Integrity;
9. Honor;
10. Responsibility.

It is interesting to see that the tenets of the Protestant Ethic correspond with the spirit of capitalism. Max Weber, in his publication *The Protestant Ethic and the Spirit of Capitalism* (originally published in 1905), argues that the Protestant Ethic provides capitalism with the moral energy to succeed. This is

---

[22] It was common for early Christians, during the Dark Ages to the Middle Ages, to engage in self-torture. Some would fast, wear sack cloths, and place pebbles in their shoes. Any pain that one bears on this Earth will lead to rewards in the next.

John Calvin (1509–1564). **John Calvin came up with the concepts of "Predestination" and the "Protestant Ethic," which drive capitalism as an economic force.**

best illustrated by the fact that Protestant countries are generally more successful in capitalism compared to non-Protestant nations.

Democracy

Democracy is not a new governmental model, but it is a relatively new phenomenon in the course of human history. Democracy was formulated in the time of the Greek city-states approximately 2500 years ago, but it failed to take root. Instead, European society remained feudal for centuries, bringing forth the question of why democracy remained dormant for thousands of years.

The reason here is simple: democracy did not have the market system to support it. Capitalism provided the base for democracy, and the gradual shift in political ideas was due to the shift in the market system. Feudalism, best suited for agrarian societies, did not have the dynamics to support democracy.

For one thing, feudalism called for stratification and limited social mobility. Power rested in the hands of a few, and one's social position was generally ascribed. The concept of individual rights and rule of the people would have destroyed the economic system. Technological advancements brought changes in the market system, and changes in the market system lead to changes in philosophical ideas. The rise of individualism and free competition called for a new political model, and democracy was it.

With the rise of capitalism, Europe saw the demise of absolute monarchy and the fall of the aristocracy. The Glorious Revolution (1688) in England ended absolute monarchy and introduced constitutional monarchy. Likewise, France had the French Revolution (1789), which saw the decapitation of King Louis XVI and his queen, Marie Antoinette. With the advancement of capitalism, monarchs no longer ruled, as the market system no longer supported absolute rule.

The values of democracy and capitalism are similar, as both expound individualism and the development of self-interest. Like capitalism, democracy has the mechanism to serve the public good. It is in the interests of those in power to serve the interests of the population, as failure to do so will result in politicians being voted out of office. Hence, in order to protect their self-interest, politicians must look out for others. Like capitalism, democracy promotes total competition.

Individualism

Unlike democracy, individualism is a relatively new concept in the course of human history. The word "community" can be traced back to the 14th century, while the word "individualism" goes only as far back as the 18th century (Kivisto, 2004). As a by-product of the Age of Enlightenment, the cultural value of individualism is driven by the capitalist money market economy.

Supported by the philosophy of Rationalism, German Idealism, and British Utilitarianism, individualism is seen as a characteristic of the modern world. In the publication *Democracy in America* (originally published in 1853), Alexis de Tocqueville argued that individualism was inevitable in the modern age.

In an age driven by capitalism, Tocqueville argues that men are the best judges of their own interests. In his nine-month tour of America (1831–1832), Tocqueville studied the American penal system. He predicted that America would be the next power, because the country was founded on a value system that supported capitalism to the fullest. Democracy and capitalism work hand in hand, and the cultural value that individualism provides acts as a catalyst.

Unlike any other country in the world, America was founded on the value of individualism. This is best illustrated in the United States Constitution, whose major premise is to protect the rights of the individuals. Tocqueville, however, had reservations, as he stated:

> In the periods of aristocracy every man is bound so closely to his fellow citizens, that he cannot be assailed without their coming to his assistance. In ages of equality every man naturally stands alone, he has no hereditary friends whose cooperation he may demand— no class upon his sympathy he may rely: he is easily got rid of, and he is easily trampled with impunity (Tocqueville, 2000; pp. 876–877).

Coming from a tradition that was founded on communalism, it is easy to understand why Tocqueville had reservations about individualism as a cultural

The French Revolution (1789). **Many historians argue that the French Revolution was the result of social transformation among the French populace. Would the French Revolution have occurred if not for the Industrial Revolution and the rise of capitalism?**

Picture by Michael Reeve (2003). To this day, the mummified body of Jeremy Bentham sits in the boardroom of University College of London, England. As predicted, the utility of the body is still served: it has become a popular tourist site.

science and technology, changes in the market system acted as the catalyst for change. Like dominoes, traditional economic, political, social, cultural, and religious values gave way to new ones. The changes were multifaceted and affected all aspects of society. Confronted with new challenges, society could no longer use old values to tackle the new problems.

Changes in cultural, political, and philosophical views complemented each other—more importantly, they supported the mechanics of capitalism. The changes, however, were too rapid, and people feared that the breakdown of society would result. It was a period of fear and uncertainty, as people tried to make sense of things.

This was the period where sociology became a discipline, applying scientific methods to explain the social phenomena in question. Sociologists like Karl Marx, Emile Durkheim, Max Weber, and Georg Simmel tried to decipher the changes brought about by the Industrial Revolution and capitalism—individuals who laid the cornerstone for a fledgling discipline. The following chapters will illustrate this further by discussing the theories of Marx, Weber, Durkheim, and Simmel in greater detail.

value. Like most social philosophers of his time, there was a fear of social disintegration and the loss of social solidarity, as the departure from communalism led society into uncharted territories.

Conclusion

The social changes that came about during the Industrial Revolution were inevitable. Precipitated by

Karl Marx (1818–1883)

The Idealistic Humanist

Karl Marx is often misunderstood, especially by those who are unfamiliar with his works. Often associated with the oppressive regimes of Josef Stalin, Mao Tse Tung, and Pol Pot, Marx is mistaken for a symbol of evil. The Cold War (1945–1989) may have contributed to this misperception, especially when the Soviet Union was often described as the "evil empire." Many saw the dismantling of the Soviet Bloc in 1989 and the subsequent fall of the Soviet Union in 1991 as testament to the failures of communism and the fallacy of Marx's ideas. However, is this assessment fair?

To answer the question fairly, it is important to understand the life of Karl Marx, the sociopolitical climate of his time, and the circumstances behind his views on capitalism. In reality, Marx was a humanist who took into consideration the welfare of the downtrodden and exploited. He witnessed the negative effects of capitalism and devoted his entire life trying to educate the masses about it.

Marx was an advocate for workers' rights. We owe things we take for granted, such as minimum wage, the 40-hour work week, time-and-a-half for overtime, work safety, workers' compensation, and child labor laws to Marx. Most western European nations currently adopt a mixed-model approach, blending capitalism and socialism together, with government-run health care, education, public housing, and transportation—all ideas conceived by Marx.

Karl Marx (1818–1883). **Often mistaken as a symbol of evil, Marx was a humanist who championed the oppressed and exploited. He dedicated his entire life to educating people on the evils of capitalism.**

The Life of Karl Marx

Karl Marx was born on May 5, 1818, in Trier, Germany. Marx came from a well-to-do Jewish family, who converted to Lutheranism in order to escape the anti-Semitism pervading the country at that time.

The birthplace of Karl Marx in Trier, Germany.
Picture by Stefan Kuhn

His father, Heinrich, was a lawyer who owned several vineyards. Marx had a very good relationship with his father, who was his confidant, and they both kept in constant touch with each other through letters while Marx was in college. Little is known of Marx's mother, Henrietta, or the role she played in his life (Wheen, 2000; Morrison, 2006).

There is little information on Marx's early childhood, save for the fact that he was a prankster who forced his sisters to eat mud pies and that he was educated in a private institution until 1830, when he enrolled at Trier High School. The headmaster there, Hugo Wyttenbach, was an acquaintance of Marx's father (Wheen, 2000).

At the age of 17 in 1835, Marx enrolled at the University of Bonn with aspirations to become a lawyer like his father. Marx was exempted from military service when he was 18, due to a chest condition, though many believed he exaggerated his ailment (Wheen, 2000; Kivisto, 2004).

Marx was a quick learner, but his behavior was self-destructive. Marx had a taste for "revelry" and "roughhousing." Marx was, in essence, an "intellectual thug"—he had a propensity for bullying people with his intelligence by making them look stupid. He would argue with professors openly in class, and at times, win his arguments (Wheen, 2000).

Marx's intelligence may have led to his arrogance, as he was one who constantly skipped classes. He drank heavily and was a member of the Trier Beer Club, whose members came from his hometown. Needless to say, Marx got into numerous fights. It was only due to the intervention of his father that the local authorities decided not to press charges (Wheen, 2000).

Marx was also an avid fencer and spent much of his time fencing. Most of his opponents were people he offended, and one opponent eventually got the better of him by slashing a scar on his face. In time, Marx's behavior became a cause for concern, and his father[1] was only too happy to see his son transfer to the University of Berlin, where the environment was more conducive to academic pursuits (Craib, 1997; Wheen, 2000; Kivisto, 2004).

Marx was captivated by the philosophy of Georg Wilhelm Friedrich Hegel[2] and tried very hard to stay away from studying philosophy[3] during his first year at the University of Berlin. Marx was introduced to "the Doctors' Club," a group of Young Hegelians in 1837. It was at this time that Marx became a Young Hegelian and changed his major to philosophy, much

---

[1] The dean at the University of Bonn wrote a formal letter to Heinrich Marx, detailing the exploits of his son. For fear of embarrassment, Heinrich transferred his son to the University of Berlin,: which was a drop in standards and prestige (Wheen, 2000; Kivisto, 2004).

[2] Marx read everything Hegel had written (Wheen, 2000).

[3] He was still majoring in law.

to the chagrin of his father, Heinrich, who was then ill with tuberculosis[4] (Wheen, 2000).

The objective of the Young Hegelians was to establish their philosophy by infiltrating the academic establishment (Wheen, 2000). Being a member of this group proved costly to Marx's career. He was blacklisted and was unable to obtain a faculty position upon graduation.

Marx did his coursework at the University of Berlin,[5] but obtained his PhD at the University of Jena. Marx decided to submit his dissertation on the philosophy of Democritus and Epicurus to the institution, since they had a reputation of granting PhDs without delay or a dissertation defense. Nine days after submitting his dissertation, Marx was awarded his PhD on April 15, 1841 (Wheen, 2000).

As a Young Hegelian, Marx was unable to secure himself an academic position. Instead, he made his living as a freelance journalist. Marx was radical in his views and had the propensity to write against the establishment and those in power. He also had the uncanny ability to attack those who funded the paper that hired him, and in the process Marx's radicalism caused him to live in exile. Marx left Germany for Paris, then Brussels, later back to Cologne, and finally to London (Craib, 1997; Wheen, 2000, Kivisto, 2004; Morrison, 2006).

Marx's exile gave him the exposure to ideas that later laid the foundations of his theory. Germany provided Marx with the building blocks of Idealism, particularly the philosophy of Hegel.[6] Marx got first-hand exposure to socialism—the foundation of his theory—in France (Kivisto, 2004; Morrison, 2006).

Marx took up the cause of workers in Brussels when the Communist League requested that he write a manifesto for their cause. It was here that Marx, along with his good friend Friedrich Engels, wrote *The Communist Manifesto* (originally published in 1848) (Craib, 1997; Wheen, 2000; Kivisto, 2004; Morrison 2006).

Marx finally mastered the theoretical perspectives of Adam Smith, Thomas Malthus, and David Ricardo (Kivisto, 2004). He spent hours at the British Library in London going through reams of paperwork by the respective authors, trying to understand the mechanics of the capitalist system. Unlike Adam Smith, Marx saw the breakdown of the capitalist system firsthand, with urban overcrowding, poverty, homelessness, latchkey children, long work hours, low wages, hazardous work conditions, and the unequal distribution of resources.

Marx spent most of his own life in poverty,[7] living in a small apartment in the Soho area of London. He was supported by Engels, who owned a mercantile company in Manchester. Marx applied for British citizenship but was rejected due to his "affiliation with the communists." Marx died the way he lived, a person without a country, on March 14, 1883. He was buried in Highgate Cemetery on March 17, 1883 (Wheen, 2000).

Theoretical Perspective

Marx wanted to break away from the prevailing thought of speculative philosophy and wanted to focus on the material aspects of society in his analysis—turning Hegel's theory on its head in the process. Unlike Hegel, who believed that it was ideas that shaped society, Marx took a materialistic approach in his analysis, arguing that it is material conditions that shape human history and not ideas.

---

[4] Heinrich Marx died in May 1838. Marx did not attend his father's funeral as he "had better things to do" (Wheen, 2000).

[5] During his three years at the University of Berlin, Marx was seldom in class and was constantly broke (Wheen, 2000).

[6] Marx vowed to turn Hegel's theory on its head. This was achieved by Marx's materialistic outlook on society,; where he believed that it was material conditions, and not ideas, that shaped a person's reality.

[7] Marx did lose a child to starvation (Wheen, 2000).

Marx believed that social relations are shaped according to the economic arrangements of the society, where people define their reality according to material conditions they have at their disposal. In *Das Kapital* (*Capital*), Volume 1 (originally published in 1867), Marx broke society down into two components: the Infrastructure and the Superstructure.

The Infrastructure is the base or the Mode of Production. Within the Infrastructure, there are two subsections: the Forces of Production and the Relations of Production. Forces of Production include variables such as factories, machines, raw materials, and natural resources, while the Relations of Production encompass the ownership of the Forces of Production, and who benefits from the economic arrangement.

In this case, it is the bourgeoisie who have capital and own the Forces of Production, and the proletariat, people who have only their labor to contribute to the relationship. To Marx, it is the bourgeoisie who benefit from the economic arrangements, while the proletariat are exploited for their labor.

In Marx's view, the Infrastructure and the Superstructure are directly related. Direct causes come from the base, where changes in the Infrastructure will lead to changes in the Superstructure. Therefore, human thoughts and actions are shaped by the economic base—reinforcing that technology acts as a catalyst for social change.

The mystery behind capitalism during the time of Marx was obvious. How could countries like Great Britain, a benefactor of the Industrial Revolution and capitalism, with such immense wealth and resources, have so many poor people? Further, why are the proletariat—the backbone of production—so poor, while the bourgeoisie accumulate all the wealth? The contradiction behind capitalism is obvious: the more the proletariat work, the poorer they get, while the bourgeoisie get richer.

Marx attributed the problem to the economic arrangements of capitalism, where workers are exploited through the means of production. This is achieved

The grave of Karl Marx, located at Highgate Cemetery in London. His grave is visited by many, and it is treated like a shrine.

through the Labor Theory of Value, where profit is extracted through labor. According to the Labor Theory of Value, the value of a product is based on the labor invested in it.

Marx describes two types of Capital for the Forces of Production: Constant Capital, investments in machines, raw materials, and technology; and Variable Capital, the portion of the capital that goes into labor. There are two possible ways of generating greater profits: Invest in constant capital by upgrading machines and technology, so that more can be produced at a much quicker rate. This, however, would lead to higher production costs.

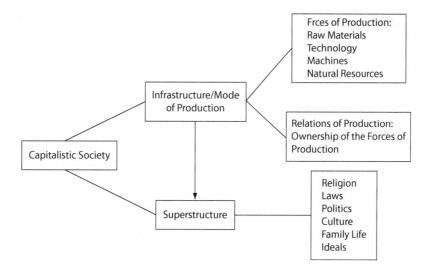

Figure 9.1 Karl Marx's Model of Capitalistic Societies

The other way is to extract more from Variable Capital. Profit in this case is (Necessary Labor + Surplus Labor Time). Surplus labor time can be extracted by lowering wages, speeding up production, working longer hours without increasing pay. Hiring women and children were also options, as they were paid lower wages. Hence, when it comes to capitalism, workers are exploited for their labor.

In his essay *Wage, Labor, and Capital* (originally published in 1849), Marx makes the argument that workers are also exploited in the marketplace. Three types of wages are mentioned: Nominal, Real, and Relative Wages.

Nominal Wage is the wage at face value, the money price for labor. This is the wage for its name's sake. Regardless if it is 1840 or 2010, $200 is still $200 by name. Of course, the value of $200 is different during their respective time periods, and this is addressed through Real Wage.

Real Wage is the wage as a unit of exchange in relation to other commodities in the marketplace. This is purchasing power: How much can you buy in the market for that amount of money? Real Wage, however, can depreciate if the wages cannot keep up with the inflation rate. Take the following as an example of how the longer one works, the poorer one gets every year:

A faculty member working at a prominent university has an annual pay increase at 3.3%. However, the average annual inflation rate of the country is 5.5%. With every year the faculty member works, the poorer he or she gets, as the pay raises do not keep up with the inflation rate. To Marx, however, the exploitation is best exemplified through Relative Wage.

Relative Wage is the share of direct capital with labor. If production increases by 30%, then each worker should get a 30% pay raise. This, however, does not occur; as profit returns to the hands of the owners of the Forces of Production. Thus, the evils of capitalism are clear: the proletariat are exploited, not only in the workplace, but also in the marketplace, and it is the bourgeoisie who benefit from the economic arrangement of society.

In his earlier writings, Marx worried about the decline in human relationships as a result of capitalism, as humans were relegated to becoming mere appendages to the machines. Through the extensive division of labor in the factories, people were no longer connected to the products they produced. Marx described this phenomenon as "Commodity Fetishism," where there is a loss of a sense of skill,

In order to lower labor costs, children were hired to work since they were paid considerably less and were easier to control. Many children were subjected to working as long as 16 hours a day. Above is a picture of children who worked in coal mines, which was extremely dangerous work. Childhood as the age of innocence did not exist for the working class. Karl Marx was against exploitation like this.

achievement, and specialty through the division of labor. In the process, alienation results when people feel they are no longer in control of their own destiny. Marx devoted his entire life trying to educate people on the evils of capitalism and saw the proletariat as the agents of change.

The Communist Manifesto (originally published in 1848), is the best summation of Marx's theoretical perspective, particularly the first chapter. Until his death in 1883, Marx made very few revisions to the text, a testimony that the work stood the test of time.

Consistent with Hegelian Dialectics, Marx divided capitalistic society into two major groups: the Bourgeoisie and the Proletariat. The bourgeoisie are those who have capital and who own the means of production, while the proletariat are the workers, who have only their labor to offer in the relationship.

Based on economic arrangements, the bourgeoisie are the benefactors of the system, while the proletariat are the exploited. This arrangement will not change as long as capitalism exists. Marx predicted the demise of capitalism,[8] and this can only be achieved through a workers' revolution resulting in an overhaul of the economic system and replacement with a new system called Socialism.

_____

[8] The contradiction is simple. The more the proletariats work, the poorer they become in relation to the bourgeoisie.

Marx was concerned about the dehumanization brought about by capitalism. Marx argued that workers, along with their families, had become appendages to the machines. The contradiction in capitalism was obvious: the more the proletariat worked, the richer the bourgeoisie became.

The premise of Socialism is simple: the equal distribution of wealth. This can be achieved through the following, as listed in Chapter Two of *The Communist Manifesto* (1848) entitled "Proletarians and Communists":

1. Abolition of property in land and application of all rents of land to public purposes.
2. A heavy progressive or graduated income tax.
3. Abolition of all rights to inheritance.
4. Confiscation of the property of all emigrants and rebels.
5. Centralization of credit in the hands of the State, by means of a national bank with State capital and an exclusive monopoly.
6. Centralization of the means of communication and transport in the hands of the State.
7. Extension of factories and instruments of production owned by the State, the bringing into cultivation of wastelands, and the improvement of soil generally in accordance with a common plan.
8. Equal liability of all to labor. Establishment of industrial armies, especially for agriculture.
9. Combination of agriculture with manufacturing industries; gradual abolition of the distribution between town and country, by a more equable distribution of the population over the country.
10. Free education for all children in public school. Abolition of children's factory labor in its present

form. Combination of education with industrial production, etc.

(Marx, 1987, pp. 104–105)

There is no question that Marx tried to address the social problems of his time. Issues such as urban overcrowding, homelessness, poverty, lack of medical care, and child labor were real, and there were no solutions to address the social injustices he saw—except to overhaul the economic system and replace it with Socialism. Government-run schools would eliminate the problem of latchkey children and also provide a means of social mobility.

Government control of the economy, along with the abolition of private property, was to ensure the equal distribution of resources among the masses. Marx believed that people, if provided with the right material conditions, live in happiness and harmony. This may come from the Idealistic tradition, which is based on the premise that all human beings are inherently good.

It is important to understand that Marx was not against the private ownership of one's home and consumer products. When he spoke about private property, he was referring to the Means of Production. The Means of Production should never fall into private hands—this, to Marx, was the underlying cause behind the evils of capitalism. Raw materials, machines, factories, etc. should be government owned.

Marx predicted the demise of capitalism, but instead, capitalism thrived and grew more complex. It is clear that Marx did not anticipate how capitalism would evolve to the way it is, with the rise of middle management and the middles class. Furthermore,

May Day demonstration in front of the Summer Palace in St. Petersburg, Russia (1918). **The Bolshevik Revolution saw the end of czarist rule in Russia and the rise of the Union of the Soviet Socialist Republics. Led by Vladimir Lenin, the Bolsheviks applied their own version of communism, modeled on Karl Marx. Did the Soviet Union, however, meet the prerequisites of socialism?**

Marx did take into account innovation and technology as catalysts for social change. As technology advanced, work and human relationships changed. Instead of workers revolting against capitalism, they merely adapted. Marx did not take into account politics and culture into the equation, as he concentrated solely on the means of production.

It is logical to conclude that Marx was a good economist but a lousy historian: he was good at diagnosing the problems of capitalism but his cure was too idealistic. Marx based his premise on the fact that all human beings are inherently good, and when given equal access they would live in harmony with one another. As history is a litany of class struggles, the elimination of class would end all struggles in humankind. Needless to say, this was not the case.

However, was socialism truly a failure? Some would argue that it was, pointing to the fall of the Soviet Bloc nations, China's move toward capitalism, with North Korea and Cuba's poverty as failures of

Mao Tse Tung declaring the founding of the People's Republic of China on October 1, 1949. The Chinese Revolution (1949), led by Mao Tse Tung, saw the ascension of the Chinese Communist Party in mainland China and the establishment of the People's Republic of China. Chinese Nationalists (the Kuomintang), led by Chiang Kai Shek, retreated to a tiny island named Formosa, which we now know as Taiwan. Like the Soviet Union, mainland China lacked the industrial base necessary for socialism to succeed.

Marx's vision. According to Marx, in order for socialism to work, two major prerequisites are required—a workers' revolution and a strong industrial base.

The Bolshevik, Chinese, and Cuban Revolutions were all peasant revolutions, and all the countries, including eastern Europe, had agrarian economies that lacked a strong industrial base. Hence, it is not that socialism failed—in reality, it never had a chance to start.

Ironically, it is the Western democracies that embrace aspects of Marx's vision. Great Britain, Sweden, Denmark, Germany, France, Finland, and the Netherlands all have public housing, schooling, national banks, national heath care systems, and government-run transportation. Their success could be attributed to their mixed-model approaches, blending aspects of capitalism and socialism into their economic models.

Looking back, the contributions of Marx were enormous. We owe much to him when it comes to minimum wage, the 40-hour work week, overtime pay, workers' compensation, work safety laws, and health insurance. Though a "rebel rouser," Marx was not the evil monster that most wrongly see him as. He tried to address the evils of his time, and devoted his entire life trying to educate people on the phenomenon. He was ahead of his time; had Marx lived in a different period, things may have turned out differently for him. To date, his grave at Highgate Cemetery in London, England, is well visited, while Herbert Spencer, whose grave is directly opposite, is largely ignored and unattended.

Karl Emil Maximilian Weber (1864–1920)

The Pessimistic Capitalist

Max Weber (1878).

The theoretical perspective of Max Weber is in stark contrast to that of Karl Marx. On the surface, it would appear that Weber is the antithesis of Marx. Marx departed from the tradition of German Idealism, while Weber was a firm defender of it. While Marx took on a materialistic outlook on capitalism, Weber differed, arguing that there were other causal factors that drove the system. Marx was a revolutionary calling for social change, while Weber was not. Marx called for the destruction of the capitalistic system and its replacement with socialism, while Weber felt that socialism would be more problematic,[1] and that capitalism was necessary.

Despite their contrasting views, however, both theorists were pessimistic when it came to capitalism. Marx provided a solution, while Weber did not. Further discussion will show that Weber had a sense of resignation, skepticism, and pessimism in his writings. This may be due to his personal experiences and the bouts of depression he fought during his lifetime (Kivisto, 2004).

---

[1] This is because socialism requires greater government intervention. In order to do so, greater bureaucracy is required and in the process, it becomes more inefficient.

Max Weber (1864–1920). Max Weber is known as the "tragic liberal," believing that capitalism was necessary during the modern age, but with a sense of pessimism at the same time. The above picture was taken in 1894.

Weber was not only an academic, but also an active participant in the political scene. He once admitted that politics was his first love (Kivisto, 2004). Unlike Marx, who lived his adult life as a stateless person, Weber was a staunch German nationalist who wanted to see Germany rise as an industrial power. Weber was known for his political speeches and lectures throughout the country, and was a member of the German delegates who negotiated the Treaty of Versailles in 1918 (Craib, 1997; Kivisto, 2004; Morrison, 2006).

Weber's Life

Max Weber was born on April 21, 1864, in Erfurt, Germany. His father, Max Weber Sr., was a lawyer who was very well connected with the local political establishment. Weber's sense of skepticism and resignation may have originated from an early age. Weber Sr. was a pragmatist who was familiar with the wheeling and dealing in the political arena. His mother, Helene Fallenstein Weber, was a staunch Calvinist interested in religious reforms. Unlike his father, who delved into the materialistic world, Weber's mother was an ascetic[2] (Kivisto, 2004).

One can only imagine the polarization the young child went through, being confronted with the extreme opposites of his parents. Weber's relationship with his father was tense, while his mother's influence was profound. Like every good mother, Helene supported her son throughout his academic career. There is no question that she exposed her son firsthand to the Protestant Ethic (Kivisto, 2004; Morrison, 2006).

Weber also benefited from his father's connections. As a child, Weber was exposed to the best minds Germany could offer, as his father often invited intellectuals to his home for dinner. One can only imagine the philosophical and political discussions that occurred in the process, and there is no doubt that the seeds of Weber's intellect and political fervor were sown at a very young age (Kivisto, 2004).

Weber was an astute student and graduated with a degree in law from the University of Berlin in 1889. Shortly thereafter, he got a PhD in Political Economy, writing his dissertation on medieval trading companies (Craib, 1997; Kivisto, 2004; Morrison, 2006).

Weber got his first academic position in 1893, and became a professor of economics at the University of Freiburg. It was during this time that he married his first cousin, Marianne Schnitger, who was also an intellectual. Weber later taught economics and political economy at the University of Heidelberg (Craib, 1997; Kivisto, 2004; Morrison, 2006).

Between the years 1897–1903, no academic work was produced by Weber as he fell into a deep depression. This may have been precipitated by an argument

---

[2] An ascetic is one who shuns worldly possessions and pleasures.

with his father during his parents' visit to his home in 1896.

Unhappy at his father's treatment of his wife, Marianne, the younger Weber got into a heated argument with his father and demanded that the father leave his home. His father returned to Berlin and died shortly thereafter, without any reconciliation between the two men.

It was shortly after this incident that Weber fell ill. He resigned his position and went on an extended vacation across Europe, only to produce his best works shortly thereafter (Kivisto, 2004).

Weber wrote his best work, *The Protestant Ethic and the Spirit of Capitalism* in 1905, and became an editor for a sociology journal four years later. During the same year, Weber embarked on his project, *Economy and Society*. It was also during this period that Weber conducted extensive research on religion, comparing religions of the West with China and India. In 1920 Weber wrote his last academic work, *A General Economic History*. He died the same year, leaving a trail of unpublished works (Craib, 1997; Morrison, 2006).

Weber was a modernist in social thought, bringing numerous theories together, and forming one of his own based on history, economics, philosophy, and law. Unlike Marx, who felt that theories should bring social change, Weber believed that theories should remain neutral. Weber paid attention to historical patterns in his analyses and reported the facts accordingly.

Significant in Weber's work is the theme of rationalization. Unlike Marx, who took a materialistic outlook on capitalism, Weber felt that there are other causal factors that drive the economic system. Marx saw the development of history through historical epochs. Weber, on the other hand, viewed the development of history through the process of rationalization,[3] which encompasses calculation, scientific knowledge,

and rational action.[4] On the whole, Weber provided interesting insights on modern society, especially the role bureaucracy plays, and his analysis of religion and world economies (Morrison, 2006).

Weber felt that capitalism was necessary during the modern age and wanted Germany to succeed as an industrial power. The premise behind capitalism is that it allows humans to exercise their rationality to the fullest by taking a scientific worldview. However, there is a sense of skepticism, resignation, and pessimism in Weber. This is best illustrated in Weber's discussion on bureaucracy (Kivisto, 2004).

The "Iron Cage" of Bureaucracy

Throughout the development of rationalization in history, Weber mentions three forms of legitimate domination: Traditional, Charismatic, and Legal Rational. Simple societies embrace traditional domination, and as rationalization evolves, it moves to charismatic and finally legal rational domination—a characteristic of industrial societies.

Traditional Domination (Authority) deals with the "way things have always been": traditions that have been passed down from one generation to the next. Reverence for one's parents, elders, religious leaders, healers, and royalty are some examples of traditional domination. The power base of traditional domination is reinforced and legitimized by religious and cultural components, where explanations are attributed to mysticism and spiritualism.[5]

Charismatic Domination (Authority) is based on charismatic leaders,[6] leaders endowed with

---

[3] This is where societal—along with individual—actions are oriented toward technical procedures and rational actions.

[4] Seeking the optimum means to any given end. "Means," in this case, encompasses techniques and strategies, while "ends" deals with one's goals.

[5] Roman emperors such as Caligula and Nero took on divine characteristics. Likewise, the emperor of China was known as "the Son of Heaven."

[6] Weber believed that charismatic leaders in industrial societies are most effective during times of crisis. Once the

Big bureaucracies: the irrationality of rationality. Administrative burden in Bucharest, Romania. **Picture by Pizzaros (2009). Max Weber was against socialism since it requires greater government intervention. Greater government intervention would lead to greater bureaucracy, which in turn, creates greater inefficiency.**

unique gifts,[7] "supernatural"[8] abilities, and the acumen to attract and lead, especially during times of crisis. Throughout history, charismatic leaders usually experience a "revelation" telling them of their mission. Moses, for example, had the burning bush,

St. Paul "saw the light" on the road to Damascus, Constantine the Great had a vision of a burning cross in the sky before the Battle of Malvian Bridge, and Adolph Hitler had his vision of his 1000-year Reich while in Landsburg Prison. In general, charismatic leaders speak about liberation, freedom for the oppressed, and a greater kingdom to come. Charismatic leaders do take on traditional domination once their power has been consolidated. King David, Constantine the Great, and Genghis Khan are just some examples.

Just as an Industrial-Capitalist society requires a scientific worldview, Legal Rational Domination

problem has abated, however, the leaders should step down and revert to Legal Rational Authority.

[7] Charismatic leaders usually have great oratory skill, with the ability to attract and unite people.

[8] Charismatic leaders are also able to perform miracles. Miracles may be attributed to unique skills the individual has over others—the ability to do things others cannot.

(Authority) is most effective. Legal Rational Domination encompasses fixed laws and procedures and sets the boundaries within which rulers can operate. Rulers are subject to laws, and they can be removed from office if they violate operating perimeters. Allegiance is to the office and not to the individual, and once the person leaves office, he or she no longer wields the authority previously held. In order for Legal Rational Domination to be effective, bureaucracy is required to ensure the following components: Efficiency, Predictability, Calculability, and Control.

Efficiency, in simple terms, is the optimum means to any given ends: producing the greatest number of high-quality output, at the lowest cost, over the shortest period of time possible. This is best achieved through mechanization and the division of labor.

Predictability ensures efficiency, as people know what to do and expect and where everyone is, and the roles they are supposed to play. With predictability, time is saved by avoiding unexpected contingencies, which can be time consuming. This is where we get the 8:00 to 5:00 workday, where people are at their respective posts, doing what is expected and ready to be found when needed.

Calculability deals with the ability to count and quantify things. Productivity is seen through the greatest number of output over the shortest period of time. Of course, output and time taken are quantifiable items. Benjamin Franklin's famous quote "Time is money" is a good example of calculability.

Control deals with the fixed perimeters in which one can operate. This encompasses policies, procedures, and decisions made according to the "chain of command." This ensures consistency and continuity, which, in turn, enables efficiency, predictability, and calculability.

To Weber, bureaucracy was necessary to capitalism—it is the epitome of rationalization. This, however, is where Weber's pessimism sets in. In the pursuit of being rational, human beings inadvertently become *irrational*, by building an "Iron Cage" of Bureaucracy.

Vision of Constantine the Great. **Charismatic leaders usually receive a "vision" or "calling" from an oracle. Here, Constantine the Great charges into the Battle of Milvian Bridge in 313 A.D. He saw a cross in the sky with the notation "By This Sign Conquer" in a vision prior to the battle. Constantine ordered his men to paint crosses on their shields and promised to become a Christian if he won the battle.**

With fixed procedures and chain-of-command decisions, humans are no longer empowered to make their own decisions, and what was created to help rationality becomes irrational, as bureaucracy creates greater inefficiency.

This is the main reason why Weber was against socialism. Socialism requires government intervention in the economy, which means requiring bigger bureaucracies, leading to greater inefficiency in the process. This is one explanation as to why capitalistic countries are more successful economically compared to socialist countries. Nevertheless, bureaucracy is necessary for any democratic regime, as it still requires specialists holding positions for which they are best qualified.

Weber's only solution to the stifling effects of bureaucracy is the form of government that he called plebiscitary democracies, requiring charismatic leaders using their appeal to occasionally challenge bureaucratic procedures—working within the system as the means of achieving such changes.

The Protestant Ethic

Contrary to Marx's materialistic outlook of capitalism, Weber offered another causal role that drove capitalism. Religion, according to Weber, can either impede or advance rational worldviews through their respective dogmas. Eastern religions like Hinduism and Buddhism[9] take on an ascetic worldview, where natural science is stifled through mystical and spiritual explanations. Western religions, especially Protestantism, allow the development of rationalization to the fullest, by providing it legitimacy and the moral energy to do so.

Weber noticed that the tenets of Protestantism complemented the spirit of capitalism itself. Protestantism, unlike other religions, offered "inner-worldly asceticism" compared to the "other-worldly asceticism" of other religions. Unlike the Catholics, who saw the Earth as the devil's domain, Protestants saw the Earth as evidence of God's glory, with the belief that one can experience Heaven while on Earth. One develops one's relationship with God while on Earth.

This can be achieved by following the Protestant Ethic of discipline and hard work.

Martin Luther argued that one's worldly occupation is seen as God's "calling," while John Calvin argued that the concept of "predestination" made the Protestant Ethic of hard work, discipline, patience, and frugality the moral ethos of his followers.

With Protestant countries more successful in capitalism than others, Weber argued that there are other causes driving capitalism apart from material conditions. To Weber, the Protestant Ethic allowed rationalization to develop to the fullest by providing legitimization and the necessary moral energy to do so. Other religions, however, tend to work counter to the spirit of capitalism, impeding its progress and growth in the process. Once capitalism is in motion, industrial societies no longer require the Protestant Ethic, as rationality has already been in its place.

The contributions of Weber to sociology are immense. His works laid the cornerstone for numerous social theorists to come. There is no question that rationalization drives capitalism to the fullest, but rationality, in turn, can be irrational when the system supersedes individual choices and autonomy. George Ritzer, a neo-Weberian, observes that Weber's rationalization is still present in our daily lives. In his publication *The McDonaldization of Society* (2008), Ritzer argues that Weber's rationalization is still alive today, as seen in fast-food restaurants, chain hotels and motels, from the entertainment industry to higher education—where efficiency, predictability, calculability, and control operate as the driving force.

As capitalism gets more complicated and complex through technology, bureaucracy becomes larger, encompassing almost every aspect of our lives. Do big governments with large bureaucracies serve the greater good, or do people end up being slaves to

---

[9] Buddhism and Hinduism believe that the world is a place of suffering, and one should accumulate merits through fasting and prayers for the next life. Both religions believe in reincarnation. The more merits one accumulates in the previous life, would lead to a better life in the next. The Buddhist aim is to reach the stage of "Nirvana,", where one becomes nothingness,: in the absence of pain and suffering.

the bureaucratic system? The debate rages on in our sociopolitical arena: Progressives[10] call for greater government intervention, while libertarians[11] call for smaller government and less intrusion. Weber, for one, would call for smaller governments[12] since the larger the bureaucracy gets, the more inefficient and irrational it becomes.

---

[10] Progressive are those who call for bigger government and the "nanny state,"; where the government acts as "Big Brother," deciding what is good or bad for people.

[11] Libertarians call for the return of the values of America's founding fathers, who wanted smaller government, less, intrusion, and greater autonomy of the individual.

---

[12] This was the reason why Weber was against socialism, as greater government intervention and programs would call for greater bureaucracy.

Emile Durkheim (1858–1917)

The Father of Modern Sociology

Introduction[1]

The contributions of Emile Durkheim to the field of sociology are invaluable. Known as the Founding Father of Sociology, Durkheim laid the foundation in establishing sociology as a science. Of the four social main classical theorists, Durkheim was the most sociological, placing the importance of society over the individual (Craib, 1997). Unlike the other traditional theorists who spoke on capitalism, Durkheim spoke solely on industrial societies (Craib, 1997).

One can make a strong argument that sociology was a by-product of the Age of Enlightenment where it departed from the ephemeral world of theory, which requires empirical proof to prove one's point. This may have been an effect of the sociopolitical schism that was going on in France during the time of Durkheim. That era saw the introduction of new social thoughts and ideas.

Durkheim lived during a tumultuous period in France's history, with numerous political upheavals and social transformations. Between the periods of 1870–1895, France underwent a deep political crisis, seeing its national unity dissipate in the face of modernization (Morrison, 2006).

Due to the polarization between individual autonomy and collective unity, social philosophers and academics tried to salvage France's national unity in 1880 by focusing on two revolutionary ideas: the stress on science and social progress that developed from the natural sciences; and individualism. They believed it was important to depart from abstract ideals of philosophy and study the problems of society through scientific methods modeled from the natural sciences such as biology and chemistry (Craib, 1997; Morrison, 2006).

The country promoted educational and political reforms, bringing about a new philosophical perspective called "Positivism." Consistent with the French tradition of communalism, Durkheim took a strong anti-individualistic stance in his works, stressing the power of society over the individual (Craib, 1997; Morrison, 2006).

Early Life

Durkheim was born in Epinal, France, on April 15, 1858, to a traditional Jewish family with a modest income.

---

[1] The theoretical perspective of Emile Durkheim falls under the tradition of Structural Functionalism. Throughout Durkheim's works, there are strong emphases on integration, equilibrium, and order.

His paternal grandfather and his father were rabbis, and as a child, Durkheim aspired to follow in their footsteps in the religious order. Durkheim's mother supplemented the family's income by working outside the home (Craib, 1997; Kivisto, 2004; Morrison, 2006).

As a child, Durkheim was well behaved and disciplined, and he excelled in school. Some time was spent at a rabbinical school, and Durkheim had a change of heart midstream and decided not to follow the family tradition. This opened the way for Durkheim's academic progress, and Durkheim pursued an academic career at a young age. Durkheim's academic pursuits were hampered by his family's financial situation and his father's illness, but the persistence and perseverance of the young man became his saving grace (Craib, 1997; Kivisto, 2004; Morrison, 2006).

In 1879 Durkheim enrolled in the Ecole Normale Supérieure. There he was influenced by Charles Renouvier (1815–1903) and Emile Boutroux (1845–1921), who encouraged him to study philosophy, history, and religion. In 1885 Durkheim was awarded a fellowship to study at the University of Berlin for a year. Due to his many publications on philosophy and social science, Durkheim was invited to teach at the University of Bordeaux in 1887. Durkheim was married the same year. It was during this period that Durkheim completed three major works, *The Division of Labor in Society* in 1893, *Rules of Sociological*

Emile Durkheim (1858–1917).

Methods in 1895, and *Suicide* in 1897.

Durkheim obtained a position at the Sorbonne five years later, and started writing *Elementary Forms of Religious Life*[2] his most ambitious work. By this time, Durkheim was firmly established as a major figure in French thinking, and he focused his attention on religion and the publication of the first French sociological journal called *L'Année Sociologique*. This is where Durkheim focused on establishing sociology as a science. The first issue of *L'Année Sociologique* was published in 1898.

Apart from his contributions to sociology, Durkheim was also a French patriot. Tragedy struck, however, with the death of his only son, André, in 1916, who was fighting for the French during World War I. This took a heavy toll on Durkheim, and he died shortly thereafter in 1917 (Craib, 1997; Kivisto, 2006; Morrison, 2006).

Influences on Durkheim

Durkheim was strongly influenced by Auguste Comte and Positivism, which called for the scientific investigation of society. Departing from traditional speculative philosophies like Idealism, Positivism called for the observation of hard facts. It was the intention of Comte to place social sciences such as history, philosophy, and

---

[2] Durkheim wrote *Elementary Forms of Religious Life* from 1902 to 1911. The work was finally published in 1912.

political economy with math, on an equal footing with physics and biology, through the use of positivistic methods. Hence, in the study of society, findings are subject to factual observation with fixed scientific methods, with the elimination of philosophical and metaphysical abstraction (Morrison, 2006).

The philosophical doctrine of Realism also had an impact on Durkheim. Realism argues that reality is independent of human perception. Contrary to German Idealism, it is external realities that shape the perceptions and realities of individuals. This was reinforced in *The Rules of Sociological Methods* (1895) and *Suicide* (1897), where Durkheim demonstrated that there is a reality that exists outside the individual (Morrison, 2006).

Restraints on the individual are impositions of society and not individual choices, going against the individualistic doctrines of Thomas Hobbes, Jean-Jacques Rousseau, Jeremy Bentham, and John Stuart Mill. To Durkheim, individuals are by-products of society (Morrison, 2006). This is best illustrated in *Suicide* (1897).

Suicide (1897)

The suicide of Durkheim's friend Victor Hommay may have played a contributing factor in writing this book. Suicide[3] was a serious moral problem of the time, and many viewed suicide as an individual choice and act of destruction. Durkheim, however, showed that suicide had social implications, indicating how external realities can affect individual perception and choices (Craib, 1997; Kivisto, 2004; Morrison, 2006).

Studying the suicide rates of Europe, Durkheim noticed a relationship between suicide rates and religion, marital status, geographical location, etc. Other variables also include such things as sudden changes in the social environment as an economic crisis. In his discussion of suicide, Durkheim mentions four

types: Egoistic, Altruistic, Anomic, and Fatalistic (Durkheim, 1979).

Egoistic Suicide[4] occurs when there is too much individualism—individuals who are not connected with society and who are thrown into a different stratosphere of it. In this category, people have inadequate connections with society and few social obligations (Durkheim, 1979).

Altruistic Suicide,[5] on the other hand, is the extreme opposite of Egoistic Suicide, where there is too much integration. People in this category sacrifice their own life for the sake of others and the greater good. This is where integration is too strong, to the point that individualism and individual needs are second to the collective (Durkheim, 1979).

Anomic Suicides occur due to a sudden change of events like the death of a loved one or a stock market crash, where individuals lose a huge sum of money. Fatalistic Suicide, according to Durkheim, is no longer consequential to industrial societies. Durkheim gave the example of the Indian ritual of Suttee, where the widow is obligated to throw herself into the funeral pyre of her dead husband as it burns. The British put an end to this practice when India became a colony (Durkheim, 1979).

From the discussion on the various suicide types, it is clear that society does have a role in determining the individual acts of suicide, especially when there is too much or too little social integration, or when there are circumstances outside the control of the individual. This is further reinforced by empirical data, when Durkheim studied the suicide rates of industrial

---

[3] Durkheim defines suicide as an indirect or direct act with the knowledge that the end result is death.

[4] Music stars such as Janis Joplin, Jimi Hendrix, Elvis Presley, Kurt Cobain, and perhaps Michael Jackson can fall into the category of Egoistic Suicide, though arguments can be made otherwise. With too much wealth at their disposal, they were no longer connected with society and engaged in self-destructive behaviors.

[5] Martyrs fall into this category, as they give their life for a greater cause. A woman jumping in front of a bus to save her child would also qualify, as she gives her life for someone else.

Europe. Discussion will cover three of the many examples provided by Durkheim (Durkheim, 1979).

Durkheim saw a relationship between suicide rates and geographical locations. Comparing urban and rural suicides, Durkheim noticed that suicide rates in rural areas were higher compared to the cities. This was because there was less social interaction in the countryside, and thus less social integration. This was due to the population density in the cities, along with interdependence in modern societies, where one relies on others to operate on a day-to-day basis. Furthermore, interaction rituals like lining up at a train station, etc. show elements of social cohesion and integration. People in the countryside, on the other hand, are less reliant on others (Durkheim, 1979).

Suicide (1877) by Edouard Manet. **Is suicide an individual choice, or does it have social implications?**

The relationship between suicide rates and gender was also evident, with males committing suicide more often than females. The reason behind the phenomenon was obvious: women have greater social obligations compared to men. Males are more individualistic, while women are more social and are socialized to put others before themselves. With greater obligations and integration, women are less likely to commit suicide (Durkheim, 1979).

Suicide rates between religions proved once again the importance of social integration, connectedness, and identity. Comparing the suicide rates of Judaism, Catholicism, and Protestantism, Protestants had the highest suicide rates, with Catholics second, and Jews with the least (Durkheim, 1979).

Of the three religions, Judaism is the steepest in tradition, with its history dating to the time of Moses.

Judaism has numerous festivals, rituals, and ceremonies, all of which are interaction rituals, providing members with a sense of connectedness, collectivity, and identity. Though Catholicism has rituals and ceremonies, they are not as intricate and elaborate, and the sense of traditionalism is not as deep as in Judaism. The theology of both Judaism and Catholicism[6] is based on the collectivity (Durkheim, 1979).

The theology of Protestants, on the other hand, encourages a direct relationship with God, without reliance and dependence on the collectivity. Furthermore, Protestantism is not steeped in tradition

---

[6] Apart from one's relationship with God, Catholics also seek intercession from the Virgin Mary and patron saints. Each patron saint specializes in a particular area. For example, if you are a teacher and need help, you can seek intercession from St. Anne, the patron saint of teachers.

and has fewer rituals and beliefs compared to the other two religions. With less emphasis on the collectivity and interaction ritual to foster integration, the connectedness with society among Protestants is weaker—hence, the greater propensity to commit suicide (Durkheim, 1979).

In the study of suicide, Durkheim saw a delicate balance between individuals and society.[7] Problems arise when individual activities and beliefs take precedence over collective bonds. Durkheim proved that suicide, thought by many to be an individual act of self-destruction, has social implication—proving society's dominance over the individual (Durkheim, 1979). This is further reinforced by Durkheim's *The Division of Labor in Society*.

The Division of Labor in Society (1893)

The Division of Labor in Society (1893) is a systematic formulation of the transition from pre-industrial to industrial societies, discussing the social changes that transpired. Pre-industrial societies are bonded with the collectivity through customs, culture, and religion. Industrial societies broke away from traditionalism, and social relationships changed, with a greater propensity to interact with strangers (Durkheim, 1997).

There was little division of labor in pre-industrial societies, and if there was any, it was generally defined through strict gender lines. Pre-industrial societies consist of clans, tribes, and villages, which Durkheim calls "Segmented Societies." Self-reliant, they are bonded together by a "collective conscious," where there is a tight grip on the individual. Individuals in segmented societies are tied down by customs and

tradition, and one's allegiance is to the collectivity and not to oneself (Durkheim, 1997).

With the increase in specialization and compartmentalization of work, industrial societies are defined by complex social structures. The division of labor, in this case, is refined, with greater interdependency with others. With traditional norms and values weakening, there is an increase in individual autonomy, and society is now held together by the division of labor (Durkheim, 1997).

In many ways, Durkheim appeased the concerns that others had with the rise of individualism and the fall of traditionalism. Durkheim argued that with societal changes, the bonding agent that holds society together changes as well. Though traditional norms and values have waned, it is the division of labor that bonds society together. Industrial societies create new forms of mutual interdependence. No matter how individualistic one may feel, one cannot escape the fact that one is dependent on others. Thus, the division of labor establishes one's place in society (Durkheim, 1997).

The Elementary Forms of Religious Life (1912)

Durkheim worked on this book from 1902 to 1911, and it was finally published in 1912. By this time, Durkheim was 54 years and was well established in the French academic world. The objective of the book was to study the impact religion has on social life. Durkheim chose to study the most primitive religions to see how religions took shape and discover the true effects religion has on individuals and society (Morrison, 2006).

As established religions were contaminated by the progression of history, Durkheim chose to study the totem religions of the Australian aborigines of central and southern Australia. Once again, Durkheim showed the dominance of society over the individual, establishing how superstition, rituals, and religious ceremonies provide individuals with a sense of belonging and identity (Durkheim, 1995).

---

[7] This is the best way to understand Durkheim's Suicide (1893):. Weaker the social integration, leads to weaker collective sentiments. Weaker collective sentiments lead to weaker social integration. Weaker social integration leads to fewerer individual acts of service to others. The fewer acts of service to others, the more meaningless life becomes. The more meaningless life becomes, the greater the likelihood of suicide.

Considered Durkheim's magnum opus, *The Elementary Forms of Religious Life* (1912) was his apology of positivism and argument against the predominant philosophy of David Hume and Immanuel Kant. Kant believed that categories were a part of human mental faculties, and it is through these faculties that human beings perceive reality. According to Kant, time, space, and cause are relative as they are facilitated by "a priori" reasoning (Morrison, 2006).

Durkheim, however, argued that society has empirical reality, and that the definition of time and space is not relative, but absolute.[8] To Durkheim, society is *sui generis*—having its own unique characteristics independent of anything else. It is society that creates reality in individuals and not "a priori" reasoning (Durkheim, 1995).

As in any positive science, the main purpose of the work was to explain how external reality affects individual thoughts and actions. A religion must serve a practical purpose, otherwise it cannot last; it has to fulfill some conditions of human existence. Rituals and rites must translate into some human need, whether social or individual (Durkheim, 1995).

To Durkheim, religion is a social phenomenon, serving as collective representations expressing collective realities. Once again, Durkheim shows the dominance of society over the individual, stating that society cannot leave the categories up to the free choice of individuals without abandoning itself (Durkheim, 1995, p. 15).

Conclusion

Looking at Durkheim's writings, we can see that the importance of society over the individual is undeniable. To Durkheim, the individual cannot be separated from society, as it is society that plays a role in the individual's personal choices, preferences, and wants. Unlike Marx and Weber, who covered capitalism extensively, Durkheim spoke solely on industrial societies. True to the tenets of Positivism, Durkheim employed scientific methods, studied social facts, and reported his observations accordingly (Morrison, 2006). Durkheim laid the foundations for future theorists of Structural Functionalism, particularly Talcott Parsons and Robert Merton—individuals who contributed to contemporary social theory immensely.

---

[8] The definition of time is fixed, as society dictates that it takes 60 seconds to make a minute and 60 minutes to make an hour. It takes 24 hours to make a day, 30 days to make a month, and 365 days to make a year. There is nothing subjective here. Likewise, in the case of measurement, it takes 12 inches to make a foot, and approximately three feet to make a yard.

Georg Simmel (1858–1918)

The Academic Exile

Compared to Karl Marx, Max Weber, and Emile Durkheim, Georg Simmel appears to be unique. Though a contemporary, colleague, and friend of Max Weber, Simmel was never embraced as one of sociology's founding thinkers, nor was he placed on a parity with the "Big Three."[1] Somehow, Simmel has always remained in their shadows, treated with the same sense of marginality as when he was alive.

Simmel did not have a theory, but he was an excellent social commentator, touching on areas that were never addressed before. Simmel's contribution to sociology is significant. He is considered by many to be a forerunner of postmodernism, and he had an influence on American[2] sociological thought (Craib, 1997).

Simmel was a theorist of modern culture, promoting cultural sociology by addressing metropolitan life, along with the effects of mass production,

Georg Simmel (1858–1918). Though disputed, many theorists attributed the origins of postmodernism to Georg Simmel. His background provided him with a unique perspective of the world, addressing areas that were largely ignored during his time.

advertisements, and mass consumption on culture. This may be because Simmel spent most of his life in the city (Kivisto, 2004).

---

[1] Karl Marx, Max Weber, and Emile Durkheim are considered the "Big Three."

[2] Simmel's approach of micro sociology was brought to the United States by Robert Park (1864–1944), one of the founding members of the Chicago School. Park had attended Simmel's lectures at the University of Berlin, and he was captivated and influenced by the man. Simmel's works were later reformulated by George Herbert Mead (1863–1931), the man who laid the foundation for the theoretical perspective called Symbolic Interaction (McQuarie, 1995). The words "Symbolic Interaction" were coined by Herbert Blumer (1900–1987).

Unlike Marx, Weber, and Durkheim, Simmel's essays are challenging. They can be difficult to follow, appear disorderly (and in many ways ambivalent), with a sense of marginality and insecurity (Craib, 1997; Kivisto, 2004). At the same time, the essays are amusing, enlightening, and intriguing. One would not be wrong to describe Simmel as a theorist of the world of leisure and consumption (Kivisto, 2004).

Simmel writes as a detached observer, providing dialectical relationships and reporting on the phenomenon in question without any solution. Though most of his essays are more than 100 years old, they still stand the test of time. A sense of detachment can be detected in Simmel's writings, and this may be a reflection of his life experiences (Craib, 1997; Kivisto, 2004).

Simmel was born in Berlin in 1858 to a Jewish family, who later converted to Lutheranism to avoid the anti-Semitism of the time. Simmel's father died when he was very young, and he had a strained relationship with his mother. Simmel was raised by prominent musician Julius Friedlander, and he inherited a large sum of money after Friedlander's death (Craib, 1997; Kivisto, 2004).

Simmel was a brilliant academic, well respected by his colleagues.[3] His academic career, however, was stymied because of anti-Semitism, and he was rejected for numerous faculty positions (for which he was qualified). Simmel's association with left-wing socialist circles may have been a contributing factor as well.

Most of Simmel's academic career was spent as a "Privatdozent," a freelance lecturer[4] at the University of Berlin. Simmel was a brilliant lecturer who spoke well and had the ability to think spontaneously. He was extremely popular and drew huge crowds, attracting women, political dissidents, and eastern Europeans. Due to his radical views, some described Simmel as an inciter or agitator, and there was actually an attempt

How has money affected social relationships and subjective realities? To Simmel, money can be rational, while at the same time, irrational. In many ways, Simmel had the same sense of pessimism as Max Weber.

on his life when someone took a shot at him. Simmel finally became Academic Chair of the Philosophy Department at the University of Strasbourg at age 56, a few years before his death in 1918 (Craib, 1997; Kivisto, 2004).

Unlike Marx, Weber, and Durkheim, Simmel reports as a detached observer in his essays and does not provide any solutions to any problems. He merely reports on the phenomenon in question, and leaves it at that. There is a dichotomous relationship in his essays, where he presents both sides of the issue. Many describe Simmel as a critique of modern culture (Craib, 1997; Kivisto, 2004). The staying power of his essays is evident, as discussion of his essays will illustrate.

As mentioned earlier, Simmel's essays can appear disorganized, as they can be abstract, and ideas expressing similar themes are littered throughout his numerous essays. The following discussion attempts

---

[3] Simmel was well acquainted with Max Weber.

[4] Simmel would hold lectures, and collected money at the door.

THE GREAT SOCIAL EVIL.

Time:—Midnight. A Sketch not a Hundred Miles from the Haymarket.

Illustration of prostitutes during the Victorian age.
**Simmel equates our relationship with money to a
prostitute. How is this so? The word "gay" meant
prostitute during the Victorian age.**

the Spendthrift (1907)[5] is the best example of this
(Simmel, 1971).

According to Simmel, money is instrumental,
abstract, and impersonal, and it removes emotional
attachments in transactions. In the essay *Prostitution*,
Simmel equates our relationship with money to that
of a prostitute,[6] as money serves as a "matter of fact"
and for venal pleasures. It is unambiguous and limited
to a sensual act, and all relationships are relegated to a
generic context. Hence, the world becomes cold and
instrumental (Simmel, 1971).

The essay entitled *The Stranger* (1908) best illustrates Simmel's sense of detachment and marginality.
This may be because he was always considered an
"outsider" in the academic circle, and this essay may
be Simmel's defense of his situation (Craib, 1997;
Kivisto, 2004).

In the essay, Simmel argues that a stranger, although alien to the society in question, can contribute
immensely, as he or she brings ideas from without that
are unique to the community. As the stranger is not
connected to the conventions of the society in question, there is a sense of objectivity. This objectivity,
according to Simmel, is a sense of freedom, as there is
a distance maintained from the rest of the community
(Simmel, 1971).

to bring the various themes together in his different
essays:

Interested in seeing how money affected cultures
and individual relationships, Simmel wrote two essays
describing the phenomenon: *The Philosophy of Money*
(1908) and *Prostitution* (1907). Simmel's eclecticism
is apparent in his approach, borrowing ideas from
Marx, Weber, and Durkheim.

In *The Philosophy of Money*, Simmel argues that
money can structure both our "internal" and "external" lives—influencing how we think, act, and
present ourselves to others. It also promotes a rational
orientation of the world, but at the same time it can
be irrational. Simmel's essay entitled *The Miser and*

[5] In this essay, Simmel shows how a miser and a spendthrift, both at opposite ends of the spectrum, can be both
rational and irrational. A miser hoards money in order to
create probabilities for himself. With money, he has the
probability to buy houses, cars, etc., but the probabilities
never become possibilities. A spendthrift, on the other
hand, spends because he has the possibility, but in doing
so, he deprives himself of any future possibilities. Hence, a
miser and a spendthrift can be both rational and irrational
at the same time.

[6] As a graduate student, I was asked in front of the whole
class to summarize the essay in one sentence. Unsure what
to make out of it, I blurted out the following sentence,
which got the entire class laughing: "Once you withdraw,
you lose interest."

The staying power of the essay *Fashion* (1904) is evident, and it is interesting to see how prophetic Simmel was in his analysis. There is no question that Simmel was aware of the effects of mass production and consumption on the psyche of individuals. Once again, the dichotomous relationship is expressed, showing views from both ends, and the effects it has on society (Simmel, 1971).

Simmel was right to mention that the modern world was at a "nervous age." With rapid changes affecting every facet of society, there was a sense of uncertainty as to what the changes might bring. However, the mass market in itself opens up new dimensions for the individual to explore, and this was expressed by Simmel in the essay (Simmel, 1971).

With mass production and the abundant amount of goods, the differentiation that results provides individuals with a great variety to choose from. People can express their individuality through different trends and fashions, but this sense of individuality can also be a form of imprisonment, as one's taste and preference are subject to fashion trends. Likewise, fashion is also not an individual choice, as it is structured by class divisions and is a means of social mobility (Simmel, 1971).

In essence, fashion produces a "double function." It shows one's connectedness with society, while at the same time allowing people to express their individuality. It is a way to preserve "inner freedom," as individuals can pick and choose from the variety of products available. It can, at the same time, imprison one's subjective reality since it is driven by fashion trends.[7] Most importantly, however, fashion is also one connection with the past and future[8] (Simmel, 1971).

***Fashion during the Victorian era (1880s).* Fashion, according to Simmel, can liberate or imprison the individual. It expresses one's individuality and conformity, as well as one's connectedness with the future and the past.**

From the essays discussed, one can see the staying power of Simmel's work in an ever-changing world. We can still associate Simmel's work with the issues we face today. In many ways, Simmel was prophetic in addressing how market forces and consumerism can affect individual choices and preferences, and how they shape social relationships. Perhaps Simmel's not providing a solution to the problems forces us to look within ourselves to make informed choices in a society driven by the culture of consumerism and conspicuous consumption.

---

[7] How many of us discard our clothes once theyit goes out of fashion?

[8] It is often said that if something goes out of style, keep it, because it will one day be fashionable again. This is true, of mini-skirts, a fashion of the 1960s that returned the 1980s.

Likewise, "bell--bottoms pants", a trend of the 1970s, came back in the 1990s.

Simmel's influence on American sociology was significant. Robert Park, one of the founders of the Chicago School, attended several of Simmel's lectures and was captivated by the man (Craib, 1997). Little did Simmel know, but he inadvertently laid the foundations for Symbolic Interaction: a micro-interactionist theoretical perspective developed by Charles Horton Cooley, George Herbert Mead, and Herbert Blumer.

Global Stratification

Despite India's economic growth, pockets of poverty still exist. Children are left to beg for their survival on the streets. Will economic progress lead to greater inequality? What happened to Adam Smith's "trickle-down" economics?

Introduction

Greater differentiation and specialization brought about by the Industrial Revolution have brought us to the next stage of the sociocultural evolution: postindustrial societies. The United States, western Europe, Australia, Japan, Hong Kong, Singapore, South Korea, and Taiwan are countries that fall into this category.

What distinguishes postindustrial societies from industrial societies is the heavy use of computers and any forms of high technology. Strong emphasis is placed on education, and production has moved from manufacturing to planning, marketing, and design. Due to education and career development, marriage and childbirth are delayed. In the process, fertility rates of postindustrial societies fall below replacement level, along with an aging population due to longer life expectancies.

With the outsourcing of manufacturing jobs abroad, we see the global division of labor. Countries can no longer remain isolationist, since the well-being of other countries would serve their own interests.

Picture by Steve Evans (2007)

With greater differentiation and specialization between nations, stratification and inequality have reached a global scale. This chapter provides the different theoretical perspectives explaining the global stratification and the effects it has on nations.

Theories on Global Inequality

In the discussion on global stratification, the question as to why some countries are richer than others is often posed. The question may appear simple and sometimes obvious, but to give a fair and accurate answer is difficult. For one, each country has its respective issues, pertaining to their ecosystem, history, political structure—and most importantly—economic system.

Social Darwinists would claim cultural and racial superiority as the reasons behind global stratification, while Marxists would attribute the problem to exploitation of labor and natural resources. Needless to say, there are numerous explanations behind the phenomenon.

Global stratification, simply put, is the inequality between nations in terms of wealth, income, and resources (Sanderson and Alderson, 2005). Global inequality appears in different forms, and the most important involve economic conditions and the quality of life. Indicators of quality of life include, but are not limited to, the following: Life Expectancy,

Singapore River and financial district (2007). **Singapore rose from being an underdeveloped country to a developed country in a matter of decades. The key question behind global stratification is why some countries are able to succeed in their developments, while others fail. What are the underlying causes behind this phenomenon?**

Infant Mortality, Unemployment Rates, and Gender Equality.

Another mystery behind global stratification is the fact that some countries that were once underdeveloped were able to progress, while others could not. Countries such as Japan, South Korea, Taiwan, Hong Kong, and Singapore, which once had humble origins, have become economic powers, while other countries, including Argentina, Burma, Cambodia, Kenya, and Mexico, are unable to compete at the same level. What possible explanations are there? Discussion in this chapter will cover three theoretical perspectives explaining the underlying causes of global stratification: the Modernization Theory, Dependency Theory, and the World Systems Theory.

Modernization Theory

The Modernization Theory is drawn from the European evolutionary theory that takes the position that underdevelopment is an original state predating capitalist societies. It takes the position that economic development is an evolutionary process, where the infrastructure, culture, and value systems (along with history) play an important role in its evolution.

Underdevelopment, in this case, is due to internal deficiencies, where the country lacks the infrastructure, culture, and value systems that complement capitalism and modernization. Countries in this category are generally very traditional, and have insufficient capital formation and the financial base for capitalism to develop.

Walt Whitman Rostow (1960) takes the position that underdeveloped countries are unable to generate sufficient income to reach the "takeoff" point, in order for economic development to occur. Rostow's theoretical perspective mentions five stages in the economic evolutionary process, as further discussion illustrates.

Countries are traditional in the first stage, embracing traditional values and economic means of exchange, with strong attachment to their lands (Rostow, 1960). Agrarian societies, whose primary focus of production is from the land, would fall in this category. This was Europe, from the Greek city-states to the Black Plague (1348–1350), where feudalism was the economic system.

The preconditions to takeoff occur with technological innovations in manufacturing, broadening of education, and the appearance of economic institutions such as banks (Rostow, 1960). This was Europe during the Renaissance, which saw a rise in the literacy rate (aided by the Gutenberg printing press), the departure from faith-based knowledge to scientific knowledge, the rise of innovation, and the ascendancy of merchants and traders as people of power and influence.

The takeoff stage for Europe was during the initial stages of the Industrial Revolution, approximately between the years 1750 to 1830. With the mechanization of production, mass production, consumption (Rostow, 1960), and the growth of urbanization, European society was able to sustain economic growth. This was further enhanced with the growth of population.

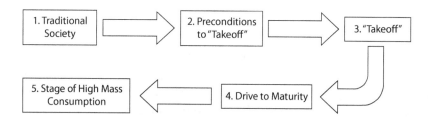

Figure 14.1. Walt Whitman Rostow's (1960) Evolutionary Stages of Economic Development

After long periods of economic progress, the "drive to maturity" occurs when technology is applied to other areas of the economy (Rostow, 1960). From the mercantile factories, technology is applied to the steel mills, shipyards, etc. This was Europe during the latter stages and earlier stages of the 19th and 20th centuries, respectively.

The last stage would be Europe after World War II to the present, as a postindustrial society. Basic necessities like food, clothing, and shelter are met. Consumption is high due to the huge variety of consumer goods (Rostow, 1960).

Rostow's evolutionary theory is consistent with most literature on the Modernization Theory. Most of it states that modernization occurs in stages or phases, and over an extended period of time. The

Diamond miners in Sierra Leone. **Sierra Leone is an example of a country with a disarticulated economy, where emphasis is placed on the diamond trade. Institutions and infrastructures facilitate the trade, ignoring other facets of the country's economy. Rampant corruption and internal unrest also plague the country.**

process of modernization is progressive and irreversible—thus, once a country reaches a stage, there is no regressing. Inevitably, modernization would also entail westernization of societal institutions and culture (So, 1990; Sanderson and Alderson, 2005).

Proponents of the Modernization Theory recommend greater contacts with developed nations as a solution. Foreign aid is essential to build capital formation and infrastructure in order for underdeveloped countries to reach the takeoff point, encouraging underdeveloped countries to imitate developed countries in order to progress (So, 1990).

Critics of the Modernization Theory argue that the theory is ethnocentric, espousing Western superiority.

They argue that terms used by Modernization Theorists such as "advanced," "modern," "traditional," and "primitive" are ideological labels applied to justify Western superiority. Furthermore, the suggestion of Western models as formulas for modernization implies that traditionalism and modernization are incompatible (So, 1990). Countries like Japan, Hong Kong, Taiwan, South Korea, and Singapore have successfully blended traditionalism and modernization in their ethos, and the syncretism of the two has worked well for them.

Others also argue that the mono-directional process of modernization posited by Modernization Theorists is not necessarily true, as the process of modernization can be unidirectional. The modernization process, in some cases, can be stopped and reversed (So, 1990), as seen in Cambodia under the regime of Pol Pot and the Khmer Rouge in the 1970s.

Foreign aid for underdeveloped nations may also be a forlorn venture, since the leaders of these countries are generally corrupt, and there is always the risk that the aid will end up in the wrong hands and/or put to improper use. Foreign domination is also another weakness of the Modernization Theory, a weakness that proponents of the Dependency Theory exploit (So, 1990; Sanderson and Alderson, 2005).

Dependency Theory

The Dependency Theory is an offshoot of Karl Marx developed by the American-trained economist Andre Gunder Frank. Like the orthodox Marxian model, the Dependency Theory focuses on economic domination and subordination. Unlike the Modernization Theory, which attributes underdevelopment to internal deficiencies, Frank argues that it is forces from without that cause underdevelopment. The underlying problem, in this case, is dependency on other nations, and it is this dependency that hampers economic growth. This is especially true when a country's economy comes under the control of another foreign power. It is because of this dependency that underdevelopment in the economy leads to underdevelopment of other areas such as political stability, quality of life, education, etc (So, 1990; Sanderson and Alderson, 2005).

One characteristic of underdeveloped countries, according to the Dependency Theory, is that they have disarticulated economies—placing emphasis on one aspect of the economy and not on others (So, 1990; Sanderson and Alderson, 2005). Sierra Leone, for example, is exploited for its precious stones, particularly diamonds, and its economy is structured on diamond extraction. The country's infrastructure is structured similarly, ignoring other areas of development that are essential. Those on the receiving end of the economic arrangement are the peasants and workers, who are generally exploited for their labor.

Another characteristic of the Dependency Theory is elite complicity, where elites from both sides collude to benefit from the situation. Dependency theorists argue that the leaders of underdeveloped countries are generally corrupt, and this corruption is reinforced—and at times protected—by Western powers to maintain the status quo, which is beneficial for both. Profits go to the banks of developed nations and not to the dependent country. As a result, capital formation is retarded (So, 1990).

Theotonio Dos Santos (1970): Three Historical Forms of Dependency

In his article "The Structure of Dependence" (1970), Theotonio Dos Santos argues that dependency is longitudinal and develops through historical stages. It begins with Western colonization and ends with the entry of transnational corporations, with the common theme of exploitation of natural resources and labor throughout.

Colonial Dependency

The entry of colonial powers had profound effects on the colonized in Asia, Africa, and the Americas. Indigenous cultures, religions, political economies, and customs were replaced with Western models, and the colonies served the purpose of providing raw materials and opening up new markets during the height of the Industrial Revolution. Raw materials were extracted from the colonies, manufactured in the home countries, and then resold to the colonies at a profit. Of course, the Westernization of the colonies inadvertently led to the consumption of Western products, which in turn led to a greater demand (Dos Santos, 1970). Consistent with the orthodox Marxian model, colonies are exploited in both the workplace and the marketplace. With

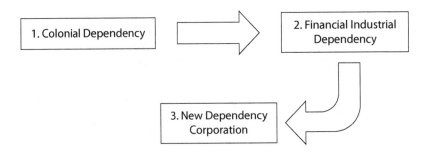

Figure 14.2. Theotonio Dos Santos (1970): Three Historical Forms of Dependency

European control of the political economy and trade, colonies became dependent on their colonial masters.

Expansion of Western Industrial Capital

This is the stage where investments in heavy technologies by Western powers are used to extract materials from underdeveloped countries. This is where the disarticulation of the economy becomes evident, when the country's infrastructure[1] is structured for one purpose only: the extraction of the raw materials in question. Investment in heavy technologies, in this case, merely reinforces the existing status quo of subjugation and exploitation (Dos Santos, 1970).

Entry of Transnational Corporations

The entry of transnational corporations, especially in the modern era, has added new dynamics to dependency. Not only is the indigenous population exploited for their land and labor, they become culturally and socially colonized to adapt to models of

developed nations. Some see the entry of transnational corporations as a form of neo-colonization, through the culture of consumerism driven by advertisements and the entertainment culture (Dos Santos, 1970).

Dos Santos (1970) argues that dependency is a developmental process, and the longer it goes on, the more dependent underdeveloped nations become. There is, however, a glaring weakness in Dos Santos's model: he fails to offer solutions on how dependent countries can become independent. Nevertheless, the theme of exploitation and subordination is present, and follows the traditional Marxian model of capitalism on a global scale.

Critics of the Dependency Theory

Critics argue that the Dependency Theory is highly abstract in the way it treats all underdeveloped countries the same. Furthermore, there is a strong overemphasis on external forces; the theory fails to closely look at internal factors like class conflicts and the existing political economy (So, 1990).

Others argue that dependency does not necessarily lead to underdevelopment. Hong Kong and Singapore, both former British colonies, have advanced and prospered economically, supporting the fact that dependency and development can work in unison. After all, the dominating presence of Western powers also presents opportunities for changes in technology, ideas, and social institutions (So, 1990).

---

[1] Roads lead to and from the mines to the shipyards. Warehouses are built to store the raw materials, offices are built for administrative purposes, and any special skill or training is catered to the extraction of raw materials. Other aspects of the country's economy and infrastructure, such as schools and hospitals, are generally ignored.

World Systems Theory

Unlike the Dependency Theory that studies the "zero-sum"[2] relationships between developed and underdeveloped nations, the World Systems Theory studies the historical dynamics of a world economy. Developed by Immanuel Wallerstein, who was influenced by neo-Marxist theories of development, the World Systems Theory echoes similar sentiments of exploitation and unequal exchange in the economic relationship (Sanderson and Alderson, 2005).

The World Systems Theory takes the position that capitalism is a world system that dates back all the way to the 16th century. It is a huge system, containing three basic characteristics: it operates with a high degree of autonomy; it is a self-containing system; and it does not depend on any other system outside of it—although there may be some interaction with regions outside of it. In essence, once in place, capitalism takes on a life of its own, with a self-propelling mechanism that perpetuates its own existence (Sanderson and Alderson, 2005; Wallestein, 2005).

Within the world economy, there is an extensive division of labor and specialization—both geographic and economic—with different economic activities allocated to different geographical regions. The system encompasses a multiplicity of societies, cultures, traditions, languages, and religion, which add greater dimension to an already complex system. According to the World Systems Theory, the world economy is made up of three components: Core, Peripheries, and Semi-Peripheries (Sanderson and Alderson, 2005; Wallestein, 2005).

The Core consists of the most technologically and economically advanced nations, whose dominance of the world economy is evident. This is where the world's wealth resides. Any production done in this area involves leading sector goods, with wage labor as the predominant type of labor (Sanderson and Alderson, 2005; Wallerstein, 2005).

The Peripheries are the least economically developed countries, with the lowest technological advances. Ruling governments in this region are weak, unstable, and ripe for revolution. Surplus expropriation by the Core, with the extraction of raw materials for export, is the economic mainstay, making the region subject to the economic demands of the Core. This region is exploited both for its natural resources and labor, where forced labor—and at times slavery and serfdom—is apparent (Sanderson and Alderson, 2005; Wallerstein, 2005).

The Semi-Peripheries contain both the exploiter and the exploited. They are exploited for their labor, but they exploit the Peripheries for their raw materials. Countries in this region engage in manufacturing, with factories producing goods and services for the Core nations. They are technologically and economically more advanced than the Peripheries, but fall short of the Core. Semi-Periphery countries have stronger governments with greater stability compared to the Peripheries, and leading sectors engage in wage labor; though coercive or semi-coercive labor systems do exists (Sanderson and Alderson, 2005; Wallerstein, 2005).

Wallerstein provides a transnational analysis of the world economy and the stratification that results in the process. Movement from the Peripheries to the Semi-Peripheries and finally to the Core is fluid and ever changing. How one country moves from one region to another is contingent on its industrialization, diversification, and ability to establish itself as a financial center, as in the case of Hong Kong. This would explain why some countries—for example, Japan, South Korea, Taiwan, Hong Kong, and Singapore, which were once peripheral and semi-peripheral nations—are able to thrive and challenge the hegemony of the United States as an economic power. At the same time, other countries such as India, Pakistan, Nigeria, etc. could not compete at the same level.

---

[2] This is a relationship where someone wins and another loses.

With the advancement of some countries, the decline of others comes to mind: will Core countries like the United States fall into the Semi-Peripheries if the current economic trend continues? This is an interesting question, as the focus of the world economy is now shifting toward Asia. Only time will tell.

Globalization

The Leveling of Cultures

The effects of globalization were apparent in the 2010 FIFA World Cup championship games held in South Africa. Not only did we see people of different nations coming together to witness a tournament of epic proportions, we saw soccer fans adopting countries to support, with people of similar nationalities supporting different countries. Apart from the fan base, FIFA's rules on eligibility reflect the effects of globalization as well.

Based on FIFA's "parentage ruling," a citizen of one country can play for another so long as one parent comes from the country the player wants to represent. An American with English parentage can play for England if he makes the grade. Hence, one can be born in one country, and yet represent another.

This is the reason why we saw two brothers, Jerome and Kevin Prince Baoteng, both born in Berlin, Germany, represent different countries during the World Cup: Jerome for Germany, and Kevin Prince for Ghana. The Baoteng brothers bring out an interesting characteristic of globalization: the weakening of borders and national identities. We currently live in a world where emigrating and migrating are commonplace, and individuals can be citizens of more than one country by virtue of birth, naturalization, or parental ruling.

Technology has facilitated the "compression of the world." A voyage that took months to travel across continents by sea now takes but a few hours. What took days and weeks to deliver now takes only a matter of hours. It is clear that technology has changed our social relationships, along with how we see the world.

Technology has also made the world a smaller place, and with greater interaction between individuals of different countries, there is a sense of worldwide connectedness. However, globalization is not restricted to the social arena, and one must look at the economic and political arenas as well.

Economic Globalization

Economic Globalization refers to the integration of the world economy through international production, trade, finance, investment, and migration. Due to the global division of labor as posited by the World Systems theory, there is an increased flow of people across borders. Along with the interdependency in the economic arena, it is difficult for countries to adopt protectionist policies.

Economic globalization raises a key question: Is the widening and deepening of the world economy a

Picture by Ben Schumin. *Protest against the World Bank and International Monetary Fund (2005).*

good or bad thing? The answer is open to debate and is contingent on the theoretical perspective one takes.

Political Globalization

With the emergence of world polity, especially after World War II, accords and alliances play an integral part in determining relationships between countries. During the height of the Cold War (1945–1989), alliances like the North Atlantic Treaty Organization (NATO) and the Warsaw Pact played an integral role in ensuring détente. The demise of the Cold War has added new dimensions to intergovernmental organizations. Organizations such as the United Nations and the British Commonwealth still exist, but what

role they play in the global market or the political sphere is uncertain. For one, the United Nations as an organization has been ineffective in sanctioning oppressive regimes for their human rights violations (as in the case of Myanmar, or Burma) and nuclear arms testing (in North Korea and Iran) over the years.

Other organizations do have their fair share of success, however. Amnesty International and Greenpeace are good examples of groups that have challenged the policies of governments and practices of multinational corporations directly rather than proceeding through diplomatic channels.

Social-Cultural Globalization

Mass production, mass consumption, advertisement driven by the entertainment culture facilitated by technology—all have influenced how people see and shape the world around them. From heterogeneity, the world is becoming more homogenous, embracing similar tastes, preferences, values, and cultural norms. This is achieved through the consumption of the same cultural products. But is the leveling of cultures positive or negative?

As mentioned, cultures serve practical purposes. Though the preservation of the human-environmental relationship is negated by technology, cultures provide people with an identity and a reference point during times of crisis and uncertainty. Would the dissolution of cultures that once held societies together be a detriment? Or would the adoption of a global culture promote global consciousness for all?

Grobalization

Grobalization refers to the imperialistic ambitions of nations, corporations, and organizations with the need to impose themselves on different geographical areas (Ritzer, 2008, p. 164). The primary objective is to accumulate power, exert influence—and most importantly—amass profits. There is no autonomy for the indigenous population, as customs and practices are one-dimensional. This raises concern for those who fear homogenization with globalization, as it destroys the unique characteristics that make a society special (Ritzer, 2008). To some, grobalization is a form of neocolonialism.

The gas leak caused by Union Carbide in Bhopal, India, in 1984, provided grist for the mill for opponents of globalization, who cited elite complicity and corporate greed as the reasons behind the disaster.

Picture by Miguel A. Monjas (2005). *Grobalization or glocalization? When Starbucks set up stores in the Forbidden City in Beijing, China, huge controversy was generated when its logo was placed on the exterior of the store. Many Chinese felt that it was a desecration of traditional Chinese culture to have a Western symbol placed in an area with great Chinese heritage. Starbucks, under immense pressure, compromised and took the sign down.*

Glocalization

Glocalization deals with the syncretism of global and local practices, providing unique characteristics in each local culture. Glocalization takes the position that the world is increasingly pluralistic and locals are empowered to improvise and adapt what is global to what is local. By doing so, they give something foreign a local flavor, catering to the needs of the population (Ritzer, 2008).

Is There a Happy Medium?

Regardless of the stand one takes on globalization, be it glocalization or grobalization, there is no denying the fact that globalization is an undeniable fact of the modern world. The economic, political, and social interconnectedness between nations is greater than it ever was before, and in time, differences between cultures and races will disappear. Though we may lose some traditional cultures, new ones are created as well. For one thing, the Internet has created new forms of language, where symbols, acronyms, and abbreviations are universal across all cultures.

Technology has also created new forms of relationships, where geographical proximity no longer determines who we meet and interact with. Perhaps we must accept that change is inevitable—and with change, we create new challenges and frontiers for ourselves that our forefathers never could have dreamed about. Perhaps grobalization and glocalization are extreme ends of the spectrum, and where we are is open for debate. Nevertheless, one must accept the fact that we must prepare for the future.

Advice for the Future

Be Prepared to Work Overseas and Relocate

With multinational corporations stretching their tentacles to every corner of the globe, one cannot be a slave to geography when it comes to finding employment. Be prepared to find employment overseas or be posted there in your professional career. Americans can no longer afford to be isolationist in their job selections. Finding a job in your hometown or close to your family may be ideal, but the economic realities of the situation may dictate otherwise. We can no longer be tied to geography. There is a world out there.

Learn a Second or Third Language

Learning a second or third language is critical in a global economy. One's marketability is contingent on the ability to speak another language, especially in areas where the economy is growing. It is beyond doubt that we have to look east to see who the next economic power will be, especially with the economy of China growing at an exponential rate. It is also important to note that companies do have owners from other countries, and the ability to communicate only enhances one's career mobility. Some academic programs have a second language requirement, and this will be a common feature among other programs in the future.

Sense of National Identity Less Defined

As seen in the Baoteng brothers, the sense of national identity is no longer defined by the country of our birth, but by how we define ourselves. A child of American parents can be born in Singapore and raised in Australia during his or her formative years. The child's socialization is Australian, nationality Singaporean, and is eligible for United States citizenship based on the parents. How the child identifies him- or herself in the future is contingent on personal choice. Some countries do allow multiple citizenships. For example, the child may be granted permanent residence in Australia and citizenship of both Singapore and the United States. The child can call all three countries home and may even have residence in all three countries. This is becoming more common among people in the Asia-Pacific region, and I predict that it will not be long before Americans experience the same phenomenon.

Be Prepared to Have Multicultural and Multiracial Children in Your Family

If this is not already happening, it may happen soon. American servicemen posted overseas often marry local women and have biracial children in the process. This is spreading in the civilian sector, especially with multinational corporations sending executives abroad. In my family of orientation, I have nieces and nephews of Indian and European descent who are scattered all over the world. Family reunions are interesting, as we have cousins who speak with different accents: some British, some Australian, New Zealand, Dutch, Indonesian, Singaporean—and my son with his Texas accent. This would have been inconceivable during my grandparents' generation, when racial and ethnic purity was important.

Adapt to the Changes

One is never too old to learn something new. With technology as the catalyst for social change, changes in technology have changed relationships in all directions. Just as in the case of Darwin's theory of evolution, organisms that are most likely to adapt to changes in the environment are most likely to survive. This is no exception in the world we live in today. With technology defining and redefining itself, we should do the same with the technological knowledge and the social changes to come.

As with the Industrial Revolution, we once again have reached a "nervous age," where there is so much uncertainty brought about by social changes facilitated by technological advances. Like Simmel, we should not try to find solutions, but pay attention to what is happening. Perhaps we should act like the detached observer he was. Just as with Marx, it is also important to understand how material conditions shape our perception of reality, and like Weber, there is also a sense of pessimism with big governments and bureaucracy running our lives.

The Social-Cultural Evolution Revisited

Cultures, no matter how strange they appear to be, serve practical purposes—the most important being the preservation of the human-environmental relationship. This relationship maintains ecological equilibrium, relieves population pressure, and ensures continuity through the generations. Environment shapes culture, and culture in turn helps preserve the environment. This is why cultures have contrasting beliefs, superstitions, customs, and rituals, as the environment would determine what is sacred and what is profane.

How well a society utilizes the environment determines at which stage of evolution they are. Though Ibn Khaldun admired the bedouins for their fortitude and the lack of luxuries, it is the sedentary societies that are generally more advanced when it comes to technology and innovation.

Technology is the catalyst for social change, and change is multifaceted. Technology changes the Means of Production. With this change, market forces change as well. This in turn shapes value systems, religion, philosophical ideas, and political systems. The Industrial Revolution, the Age of Enlightenment, the Protestant Reformation, the rise of capitalism, and democracy are all examples. What is most important here is the fact that technol-ogy changes social relationships through material conditions.

From hunting and gathering to the postindustrial societies of today, we see that technological advances lead to greater differentiation, which in turn leads to greater specialization. With greater specialization, stratification results; this in turn leads to greater inequality.

We do not have to look very far to see examples of this phenomenon. Compare the salaries of the chief executive officers of Fortune 500 corporations with that of the working poor and the answer is obvious. Likewise, look at the salaries of actors, entertainers, and athletes and compare them with the amount teachers are paid—the disproportion is staggering. If people are paid according to their merit and the purpose they serve, how can we explain such wage disparities? This was the contradiction Marx saw with capitalism, where he argued that workers are not paid their direct share of capital in terms of relative wage. Looking back in retrospect, was Marx wrong in his analysis of capitalism?

Throughout history, we see a correlation between the efficient utilization of the environment and the rise in population, due to a larger carrying capacity. This has certainly been the case since the Industrial Revolution. The global population has risen drastically since the Industrial Age. As seen in the writings of Thomas Malthus, there was a fear that the Earth's population would one day tax the carrying capacity of the environment. The fear of population pressure, however, may be alleviated in the face of modernization with its lower fertility rates. As in any social phenomenon, however, new solutions inadvertently create new problems.

In the case of developed countries, emphasis on education and career has resulted in the delay of marriage and childbirth. It is not uncommon for women to have their first child in their mid thirties or early forties. Countries such as Singapore, Hong Kong, Japan, Great Britain, and Sweden are no longer replacing themselves. Developing countries like China are also experiencing similar demographic trends, with their fertility rates falling below replacement levels. It is clear that the Chinese are experiencing the effects and repercussions of their one-child policy in the 1980s.

All the countries mentioned[1] are confronting an aging population, and the dependency ratio of these countries will rise if nothing is done to reverse this trend. Perhaps this may explain why the immigration debate is such a heated issue in the United States. In every major election, we constantly hear debate on immigration reforms, with conservatives calling for tighter immigration control and liberals calling for open borders.

Singapore has tried to reverse this trend by encouraging families to have more children, and the government has liberalized their once-stringent immigration policies to countries such as China and India. Anti-immigration sentiment, however, has grown among Singaporeans in the face of economic downturns and escalating costs. It will be interesting to see how the Singaporean government deals with the unintended consequences of their policies.

As technology is changing rapidly, it is logical to conclude that social changes will also change accordingly, in lieu of the fact that technology is the catalyst for social change. However, if these changes are too rapid, social disorganization can occur as traditional norms and values weaken. This is problematic, especially with societies that have traditions dating back thousands of years. Sociologists term this phenomenon Social Disorganization, where there is a period of "Anomie."[2]

There are two possible solutions to the problem: slow down social change and return to traditionalism. Traditionalists have called for the return of cultural values or norms, while extreme fundamentalists have resorted to sabotage by blowing up roads, plants, bridges, and buildings, with the intention of slowing social change. Such insurgencies will not end, as long as there is a clash between traditionalism and modernization. Structural functionalists would argue that only time will solve such problems.

Along the same tangent of traditionalism, what happens to cultures when they no longer serve a practical purpose? As discussed in earlier segments of the book, cultures preserve the human-environmental relationships of societies. This relationship, however, has been negated by technology, and with the progression of time, customs and rituals that once had meaning have become meaningless. Does this imply that the binding agent that holds society together is slowly dissipating, or have new ones evolved in the face of new challenges? With the leveling of cultures due to globalization and technology, the topic is open for debate. Whether this is good or bad in the long run is a matter of perspective—once again, only time will tell.

As you can see, the evolution of societies is an ongoing process. Our children will never see the

---

[1] I only mention these countries for the sake of discussion. Obviously, there are more countries in the world whose fertility rates have fallen below replacement level. They are faced with an aging population due to greater life expectancy.

---

[2] This is a term used by Emile Durkheim to describe "normlessness.".

Homeless person in Ueno Park, Tokyo, Japan. **Photo by Yeo Kok Leng (2009). This picture reflects the reality of the contradictions of capitalism. How could a rich, affluent country like Japan have so many homeless on the streets? Wage disparities, along with the rising cost of living, have driven some Japanese to live on the streets.**

world the same way we do, and their children will do likewise. When my son asked me about my childhood and the games we played, I told him that we ran, climbed trees, fought, and threw stones. He looked at me with amazement. I explained to him that computers did not exist, and that the invention of the VHS (videocassette recorder) was still a few years away. Cable television did not exist and we relied on television antennas for reception.

The only thing we could do was play outdoors, and we did not return home until dark. Mother always complained how filthy I looked, and why my shirt and pants were always torn. To me, they were

symbols of pride—a concept that my son has a hard time understanding.

As you can see, the gap between generations is growing much wider with technological innovations. Children no longer have the concept of how their parents and grandparents lived, and few can truly appreciate the trials and tribulations their forefathers went through to give them the lives they now enjoy.

In many ways, technology has made us ungrateful for the life we enjoy today. We take too many things for granted and become accustomed to the luxuries we enjoy. Ibn Khaldun said that luxury corrupts, as it destroys the fortitude that makes human strong.

Have we, in our technological innovation, written our own epitaph? For one, we have become slaves to our own creations. Can anyone live without his or her cell phone, laptop, or computer for a single day? Will this problem become worse, whereby, according to Karl Marx, we become appendages to the machines? As mentioned in the movie *Terminator II*, "The future is ours to make." We have our destiny in our own hands.

Bibliography

Abercrombie, M. S. (1994). *Dictionary of Sociology.* London: Pengin Books.

Andreski, S. (1971). *Herbert Spencer: Structure, Function, and Evolution.* New York: Charles Scribner and Sons.

Babbie, E. (1990). *Survey Research Methods.* Belmont, CA: Wadsworth Publishing Company.

Bentham, J. (2000). *Selected Writings on Utilitarianism.* Hertfordshire, England: Wordsworth Classics of World Literature.

Berg, B. L. (2001). *Qualitative Research Methods for the Social Sciences.* Boston: Allyn and Bacon.

Cipolla, C. M. (1993). *Before the Industrial Revolution: European Society and Economy 1000–1700.* New York: W. W. Norton and Company.

Craib, I. (1997). *Classical Social Theory: An Introduction to the Thought of Marx, Weber, Durkheim, and Simmel.* New York: Oxford University Press.

Creswell, J. W. (1998). *Qualitative Inquiry and Research Design.* Thousand Oaks, CA: Sage Publications.

de Hartog, L. (1999). *Genghis Khan: Conqueror of the World.* New York: Barnes and Noble Books.

de Tocqueville, A. (2000). *Democracy in America.* New York: Bantam Classics.

Dos Santos, T. (1970). The Structure of Dependence. *American Economic Review 60*, 231–236.

Durkheim, E. (1979). *Suicide.* New York: The Free Press.

Durkheim, E. (1995). *The Elementary Forms of Religious Life.* New York: The Free Press.

Durkheim, E. (1982). *The Rules of Sociological Methods.* New York: The Free Press.

Goffman, E. (1979). *Gender Advertisements.* New York: Harper and Row.

Harris, M. (1998). *Good to Eat: Riddles of Food and Culture.* Long Grove, IL: Waveland Press.

Harris, P. (2000). *Designing and Reporting Experiments in Psychology.* Buckingham, UK: Open University Press.

Hobbes, T. (1987). *Leviathan.* London: Penguin Books.

Hofstadter, R. (1992). *Social Darwinism in American Thought.* Boston: Beacon Press.

Honderich, T. (1995). *The Oxford Companion to Philosophy.* Oxford, England: Oxford University Press.

Khaldun, I. (1967). *The Muqaddimah.* Princeton: Princeton University Press.

Kivisto, P. (2004). *Key Ideas in Sociology* (2nd ed.). Thousand Oaks, CA: Pine Forge Press.

Lenski, G. (2005). *Ecological-Evolutionary Theory: Principles and Applications.* Boulder, CO: Paradigm Publishers.

Lenski, G. (1984). *Power and Privilege: A Theory of Social Stratification.* Chapel Hill: University of North Carolina Press.

Levy, M. J. (1967). Social Patterns (Structures) and Problems of Modernization. In W. Moore and R. M. Cook, *Readings on Social Change* (pp. 189–208). Englewood Cliffs, NJ: Prentice-Hall.

Lipset, S. (1963). *Political Man.* Garden City, NY: Anchor.

Lofland, J. L. (1995). *Analyzing Social Settings.* Belmont, CA: Wadsworth Publishing Company.

Malthus, T. (2008). *An Essay on the Principle of Population.* Oxford, England: Oxford University Press.

Mannion, J. (2007). *Essential Philosophy.* Cincinnnati: David and Charles.

Marx, K. E. (1987). *The Communist Manifesto.* Middlesex, England: Penguin Books.

McQuarie, D. (1995). *Readings in Contemporary Sociological Theory.* Upper Saddle River, NJ: Prentice Hall.

Morrison, K. (2006). *Marx, Durkheim, Weber: Formations of Modern Social Thought.* Thousand Oaks, CA: Sage Publications.

Payne, R. (1995). *The Life and Death of Adolph Hitler.* New York: Barnes and Noble Books.

Pope, H., Phillips, K., and Olivardia, R. (2000). *The Adonis Complex.* New York: Touchstone Books.

Ricardo, D. (2004). *The Principles of Political Economy and Taxation.* Mineola, NY: Dover Publications.

Ritzer, G. (2008). *The McDonaldization of Society.* Los Angeles: Pine Forge Press.

Rostow, W. W. (1960). *The Stages of Economic Growth: A Non-Communist Manifesto.* New York: Cambridge University Press.

Rousseau, J.-J. (1994). *The Social Contract.* Oxford, England: Oxford University Press.

Sanderson, S. K., and Alderson, A. (2005). *World Societies: The Evolution of Human Social Life.* Boston: Pearson Education.

Schutt, R. K. (2006). *Investigating the Social World.* Thousand Oaks, CA: Sage Publications.

Smith, A. (2009). *The Theory of Moral Sentiments.* Mansfield Center, CT: Martino Publishing.

Smith, A. (2000). *Wealth of Nations.* New York: The Modern Library.

So, A. Y. (1990). *Social Change and Development.* Newbury Park, CA: Sage Publications.

Spencer, H. (1971). *First Principles.* New York: Scribner and Sons.

Spencer, H. (1971). *The Principles of Biology.* New York: Scribner and Sons.

Spencer, H. (1971). *The Principles of Ethics.* New York: Scribner and Sons.

Spencer, H. (1971). *The Principles of Psychology.* New York: Scribner and Sons.

Spencer, H. (1971). *The Principles of Sociology.* New York: Scribner and Sons.

Spencer, H. (1971). *The Study of Sociology.* New York: Scribner and Sons.

Spradley, J. P. (1980). *Participant Observation.* Fort Worth, TX: Harcourt Brace College Publishers.

Tuchman, B. W. (1978). *A Distant Mirror: The Calamitous 14th Century.* New York: Ballatine Books.

Turner, J. H. (1998). *The Structure of Sociological Theory.* Belmont, CA: Wadsworth Publishing.

Wallace, R., and Wolf, A. (1991). *Contemporary Sociological Theory: Continuing the Classical Tradition.* Englewood Cliffs, NJ: Prentice Hall.

Wallerstein, I. (2005). *World-Systems Analysis: An Introduction.* Durham and London: Duke University Press.

Weeks, J. (2002). *Population: An Introduction to Concepts and Issues.* Belmont, CA: Wadsworth Publishing.

Wheen, F. (2000). *Karl Marx: A Life.* New York: W. W. Norton and Company.

CPSIA information can be obtained
at www.ICGtesting.com
Printed in the USA
LVHW062038170123
737273LV00003B/17